THE *New* Academic

A Researcher's Guide to *Writing* and *Presenting* Content in a Modern World

SIMON CLEWS

sourcebooks

Praise for *The New Academic*

"You're a scientist who's perfectly capable of talking to your fellow scientists; but how do you communicate to the outside world? How do you lose the jargon and the technical language, but keep the ideas, and your passion and enthusiasm? This book lays it on the line in a way that is accessible, understandable and, importantly, enjoyable to read.

"It should be required reading for any academic hoping to engage with audiences beyond the academy."

—Peter Doherty, Nobel Prize–winning immunologist

"I laughed...then I cried and wished I had this book sooner. Simon Clews understands the dilemmas of academics who are tasked with creating 'impact' and then don't really know what to do. This book has solid advice and great ideas for action. If you only do some of this, you will be able to tick that 'impact' box with ease. I owe Simon big time for giving me some of this advice when I started *The Thesis Whisperer* blog ten years ago—but now I know how much he was holding out on me! I recommend this book for anyone starting out as an academic, and for old hands like myself. Automatic buy."

—Inger Mewburn, The Thesis Whisperer

Also by Simon Clews

Your Time Starts Now!:
A Guide to Achieving Success in the
Three Minute Thesis Competition
(Thesis Whisperer Books)

Be Visible Or Vanish: Engage, Influence,
and Ensure Your Research Has Impact,
co-authored with Inger Mewburn
(Routledge)

Published by Sourcebooks
P.O. Box 4410, Naperville, Illinois 60567-4410
(630) 961-3900
sourcebooks.com

Originally published as *The New Academic: How to Write, Present, and
Profile Your Amazing Research to the World* in 2021 in Australia by NewSouth
Publishing, an imprint of the University of New South Wales Press Ltd.

Cataloging-in-Publication Data is on file with the Library of Congress.

Printed and bound in United States of America.
VP 10 9 8 7 6 5 4 3 2 1

I must have the best job in the world. Every time I stand in front of a room full of people to teach, I am without a doubt the least smart person in the room. Always. And often by quite a margin. And yet every single one of them—all those really smart people—sit quietly and listen to me, sometimes even paying good money for the privilege of doing so. How good is that?!

This book is dedicated to all those smart people: the scientists, artists, historians, and philosophers; the physicists, biologists, linguists, and engineers; the paleontologists, chemists, psychologists, and doctors. All of you. You have taught me a lot. I hope I've taught you something in return. Now, go and save the world and make it a better place. The rest of us are relying on you!

CONTENTS

1

GETTING STARTED

1

INTRODUCTION

In which we shake hands, exchange business cards, and ask what it means to be an academic in today's rapidly changing world.

Used these days as a less-than-complimentary synonym for academia, the phrase *ivory tower* seems to have originated in biblical times, when it implied notions of purity. Later it crops up in nineteenth-century France as a phrase associated with being a bit of a dreamer. And there are those at Oxford University who like to think of it as a reference to the towers of All Souls College, although to my eye, they are more gray than ivory.

Whichever it is, the ivory tower—the world of universities—has only recently come to take on negative connotations. Originally a place where people were happily and willingly cut off from the rest of the world in order to engage in high-minded, esoteric pursuits, these days it represents an enclave that is not so much cut off as shut off from the rest of the world. The word *aloof* appears in many contemporary definitions. And the notion of coming down from the ivory tower no longer refers to its high-mindedness but rather cynically suggests a need for its inhabitants to get their feet back on the ground and to get in touch with reality. But you're not like that, are you? You're different. Which is why you're reading this book.

Academia can be a funny place. When asked, I used to tell people that working at a university was a bit like being sent back to medieval times to work in the diplomatic corps of a far-flung principality on another continent on a distant planet in a parallel universe. The reality, of course, is much stranger than that. But I'm sure you've worked that out already.

Of course, I'm not talking about the research side of academia here. And certainly not *your* research. Your research is pure and noble and unsullied by the day-to-day vagaries of academia. It's incredible, exciting, innovative, world-leading, and all the things we expect it to be. It's just the context that gets a bit...well...odd from time to time. But what can you expect from an industry that prefers to speak in jargon or acronyms and where no one seems to be able to get by without at least four pointless meetings a day? And don't get me started on "cc all"!

The good news, however, is that what you have come (or should I say, have been conditioned) to consider normal within academia is most definitely not acceptable the moment you step outside its hallowed halls. In fact, the outside world is a very welcoming and supportive place to share your ideas and discoveries. You're going to love it.

I've spent many years now teaching written and oral communication and what is currently called "engagement" at universities all over the world. Before that, I used to spend my days hanging out with writers. Actually, what I did was organize huge literary festivals and events. It was a lot of fun and sometimes it did just feel like hanging out with writers. I once even got to chat onstage with 007 James Bond, a.k.a. Sir Roger Moore. Seriously. Talk about a fanboy moment! I also wrote for newspapers and magazines and even, in a moment of pre-internet madness, had a go at a guidebook. Before that, I did various odd (and I do mean odd) bits and pieces in film, television, and live theater. Fire eating, anyone?

And then came a turning point when a university that really should have known better entrusted me to take some of the country's brightest and best and train, motivate, and encourage them to start talking to the rest of us. What were they thinking?!

What I hope to do with this book is to show you how to share your ideas with the world outside academia. We're going to go back to school and learn how to write, then we'll start talking in a whole new way. We'll look at making the world sit up and pay attention to us, and finally we'll look at managing all this—both inside and outside the academy. There are audiences—huge audiences—out there who are eager to hear about your research and your amazing discoveries. And as I hope you'll discover if you keep reading, there are some very important reasons why you should share with them. So let's get on with it!

2
ACADEMIC 2.0

Time to set the scene for the all-new, outward-facing version of academia and look at how we can grow and develop those "transferable skills" of yours.

Education is big business these days. In the U.S., nearly four million people are employed at just under six thousand institutions across the country. As an export earner, the sector generates well over $40 billion a year—not an insignificant figure by any means—and there are about 21 million people with master's degrees and 4.5 million doctoral degree holders in the country. If only they'd all buy this book!

Over the years, academia has weathered more than its fair share of crises. Unfortunately, the world facing young up-and-coming researchers is a good deal less certain than anything their predecessors ever had to face. But the situation is not hopeless. It just means academics looking optimistically toward the future also need to start looking outside the academy. And if you need a label for this new outward-facing academic, what better label than "the new academic"!

So what does it mean to be a new academic?

Let's be clear right from the start: it doesn't change the academic side of your world. You are still the expert researcher working tirelessly to make new discoveries in your field, to advance the sum of human knowledge, and to generally improve the lot of humankind and, all things going well, save the planet.

What does change, however, is who gets to hear about the amazing work you are engaged in and how you write and speak about it. You'll still toil tirelessly in the labs, libraries, and archives and out in the field, but it's what happens next that will change.

The academic of old would publish their discoveries in academic journals, which would be read widely—and when I say "widely," I mean by a handful of people in their field who subscribe to those journals and who probably already know about the work. As an aside, it is entirely possible that these "old academics" might also have had to pay to be published in these journals, a practice akin to what used to be quite rightly known as vanity publishing and that I have heard recently is on the rise again. Best we don't go there.

The new academic, on the other hand, still does this (although let's hope they are smart enough not to pay to be published) but takes the dissemination of their work one step further. They share. They share what they have learned with the rest of us. Over recent years, this sharing of knowledge and discoveries has had many names— knowledge transfer, knowledge exchange, and now, its current incarnation, engagement. By the time you are holding this book in your hands, it will probably be called something else, but its essence will still be the same.

The new academic also knows something that the old academic either didn't get or possibly just preferred to ignore—the fact that they have many responsibilities, all of which point toward the need or even requirement that they share. Basically, it's now part of your job. Engagement is no longer seen as a quirky add-on that an enthusiastic few do when they have the odd moment to spare but is becoming embedded in the normal university cycle of teaching and research. This, I think, is brilliant and should be encouraged.

You can't own knowledge. No one can actually own knowledge. Sure, commercial interests will try to keep it to themselves to exploit knowledge for money, and universities have whole divisions set up to make the most out of intellectual property, copyright, patents, and the like. But in its purest sense, knowledge is abstract and ephemeral and belongs to all of us.

You also have a financial responsibility. Who paid for the lab you're working in, the library you are accessing archival materials in, even the lecture theater you are speaking or taking notes in? Certainly not you. Whether it's a corporate sponsor, a generous donor, or even a grant from the public purse, it will almost certainly be someone else's money at play here and that someone else would quite like to see what they are getting for their money. The public, whose purse this money comes from, would quite like to see what they are getting for their money. Not in an aggressive, confrontational way, of course. They are genuinely interested in what you are up to and want to see that they are getting value for their money.

The new academic understands the importance of the numbers game—the return on investment or input-output ratio, if you like. A typical PhD thesis is a very good example. You put at least four years of resources and energy into this thing, producing quite a lot of blood, sweat, and tears along the way, and it is read by just six people—the five members of your dissertation committee and your mother. Now, we know your mother is probably lying when she says she's read it, but let's give her the benefit of the doubt for now. But six people? To my mind, that seems like a very small return on a huge investment. Here's a suggestion—how about you take the ideas in your thesis, rework them, and turn them into a book that, with modest success, might reach six thousand people? Or write something for a quality magazine that could be seen by sixty thousand people? Or reach out to, say, six hundred thousand people through the pages—both online and offline—of a good daily newspaper? Of course, these are just nice round numbers, but the point is an important one to make, I think.

The new academic loves to share their excitement and passion for their work. Whether it be science, art, history, languages, physics, biology, medicine, dentistry, sociology, or business, they are so taken with it that they can't not share.

We are also talking about a very career-smart move here. I have yet to encounter a university where engagement of some sort wasn't part of performance evaluation. These days, if you want promotion or tenure or—increasingly common in these days of contracted labor—just another twelve months with an office, a university email address, and a view of the quad, you need to be able to demonstrate how engaged you are.

Remember how it's not your money—how we are all using funds from sponsors, funding bodies, or the public purse? Well, we often have to acknowledge and publicly thank our supporters for their contribution to our work. And we have to do this in simple, elegant language that can be understood by anyone. The new academic knows how to do this.

When you really, really like something, you want it to go on forever. You get it with that bittersweet feeling when you finish reading a particularly good book. Academia is no exception to this rule. Which means the new academic has an important role in enthusing and inspiring the next generation of researchers. Engaging with them, sometimes while they are still quite young—in schools, for example—is key to this. And as always, you can't do this if you can't speak the language that your audience understands.

The new, engaged academic might also enjoy what I like to call lifestyle gains; once you start to talk and write about your work in the public arena, you'll find people ushering you into radio studios so you can share your ideas with large numbers of people. You might find yourself popping into wardrobe and makeup before sitting under the hot lights of a TV studio. You'll get put in taxis, taken out to lunch, perhaps even flown places and accommodated in quite nice hotel rooms. And most importantly of all, throughout all this, you'll get listened to and taken seriously. You will probably even get introduced as "an expert"—impressive or what? And unless you get really unlucky, no one is going to challenge you or try to show they are smarter than you, that they are better than you. The outside world is a very supportive place to get out there and talk.

And sometimes there are even financial gains. Once in a while, you'll actually get paid cold, hard cash to do this. That's right—there is a tiny bit of monetary gain on the cards. Of course, a few well-earned dollars for your magazine or newspaper work is never going to be enough to pay off the home loan or even put a deposit on that shack on the coast, but that's not the point. It's nice to feel valued, even if only in a small way, and it's still financial compensation for your knowledge and expertise that you deserve and have earned.

And whether you get paid or not, talking about what you do to people who want to hear what you have to say can actually be a lot of fun. Make sure you enjoy the moment.

Your newly acquired place on the public stage will allow you to shape public opinion and exert influence over public policy. Essentially, by taking part in the public conversation, you help make the world a better place for all of us. And as a respected expert, you can stem the flow of negative information if there is any and inspire critical, informed discussion and thinking. Not a bad aim to have.

And then there's your real obligation—to help those of us who don't understand the things that you do. If you don't take part in the public conversation, preferring perhaps to step back and let others handle it, you create a vacuum, and it won't be long before that vacuum is filled by others—people who probably don't know what you know, who probably don't have the public's best interests at heart, and who may even have malevolent intentions. The tobacco lobby and their sterling work in creating a smokescreen (pun absolutely intended) over the effects of cigarettes for all those years is a classic example of the public debate being hijacked. And as confused as the climate change debate is, if it wasn't for researchers in the field speaking out, we'd probably all be walking around carrying lumps of coal, grinning like idiots as the Doomsday Clock moves closer to midnight.

Importantly, the general public is actually genuinely interested in the sort of work that you do. So why not share what you do with an appreciative audience? You'd be surprised how enjoyable it is to communicate with people who want to hear what you have to say.

Of course, this list of reasons for why you might engage with the outside world is by no means inclusive. Maybe you have other reasons for stepping out onto the world stage. But I think we are all agreed that an inward-looking academy is no longer good enough, and it's time for all of us to turn around and face the rest of the world.

As you embark on this exciting adventure to become a new academic, I am going to encourage you to be brave. You will encounter huge goodwill and support, but just once in a while, you might get dark looks, raised eyebrows, mutterings of "dumbing down," or, in the extreme, the feel of cold steel between your shoulder blades. That's right: knives in the back. Don't worry. It's never anything but sour grapes and jealousy. Just be brave!

There are a lot of things you could achieve by becoming a new academic: money, media mentions, kudos and respect, acclaim, and influence. Think about which—if any—of these rewards you are enjoying now. Now try closing your eyes and letting your imagination run for a minute. What will the you of five or ten years hence look like? What will they be doing? And what rewards will they be used to receiving?

No need to tell anyone else what you see, but just fix that picture in your head. Got it? Good. OK, now let's see if we can't get you there. I am going to start by teaching you how to write.

2
WRITING

3

JUST WRITE BETTER

A long, hard look at the main tool of the trade you have as a communicator—words. Here's how to use them and how to make them work for you.

I t sounds so simple, doesn't it? "Just write better." But it really is the answer to most writing-related questions.

Let me tell you a little story. One sunny afternoon nearly two decades ago saw five hundred or so literary-minded souls crammed into a theater in Melbourne. The local writers' festival was coming to a close, and the crowds had gathered to hear their literary idol of the moment, the legendary E. Annie Proulx. Ms. Proulx was—and still is—a formidable public figure. She spoke her mind, she didn't suffer fools gladly, and—as the Pulitzer Prize judges had agreed—she could write.

The Melbourne Writers Festival was the last stop on her world tour. After a whirlwind global tour, this was the last session in the last city in the last country she would visit. She was understandably more than a little tired. After being mercilessly probed by a local literary luminary for close to an hour, all that stood between

Ms. Proulx and a fast jet home was twenty minutes of questions from the audience and a spot of book signing.

Right at the end of the Q and A segment, a brave audience member stood up and began an attempt on the world record for the longest and most circuitous question at a literary event. What seemed like hours later, she finally reached her point: "How do we"—during the course of the question, she had included herself, a writer, in that "we"—"how do we cope with rejection?" Ms. Proulx fixed her with a steely gaze, paused while everyone in the audience listened for the dropping of the proverbial pin, then paused a great deal longer, and finally leaned into the microphone and slowly uttered three words: "Just write better."

Fast-forward a couple of decades to the University of Melbourne, where I used to have panels of editors and publishers listen to pitches for book ideas from postgrads, postdocs, and early-career researchers with amazing stories to tell. In a few short minutes each, these talented individuals would detail their discoveries and how they hoped to turn them into bestselling books and then look hopefully to the industry experts for approval. In every case, no matter how convincing the pitch was, no matter how amazing the story was, one response was universal. Even the most positive reaction, including that holy grail of pitching sessions—an invitation to send something in to be read—would end with the qualification that the idea may well be eminently publishable "as long as the writing is good."

The bottom line is it's all about the writing. Good writing can be the difference between a dusty drawer of promising ideas and half-finished manuscripts that never see the light of day and a career as a published author. Let's look at how we can just write better, shall we?

So what exactly is writing? Well, writing is little more than ink on paper or pixels on a screen. It's what it represents that matters. When we write or speak, what's going on in our heads may well be in the form of text, but equally we could be seeing pictures or even grappling with highly abstract concepts. Whichever it is, our aim as communicators is to get that text, or those pictures or concepts, into the heads of our audience. And when we are writing, we only have one way of doing that; the only tools of the trade available to us are words. So we must use them carefully, respectfully, and accurately.

WHY WRITE BETTER?

Before we really get stuck into how to write better, we should probably address the question of *why* you should even bother writing better. Better writing is always more convincing and more persuasive. It will help you win the grant, get the job, and maybe even change the world and make it a better place. Better writing is also shorter, sharper, and more to the point. To use a cliché, it is effective and efficient, and in a world where we all lead busy lives, that counts for a lot. And it's much more personally rewarding; you really will feel better if your writing is better. In academia, it will help you stand out from the crowd.

The other question you should address before you start to write is what sort of writer are you? Bestselling writer John Birmingham talks of landscapers versus gardeners, and writing software Scrivener asks if you "plan" or "plunge." So do you plan what you want to write carefully and only then plunge headlong into the writing? Or do you leap in and write straightaway, then figure out the details as you go? The reality is there is no correct way of writing; there is only the way that works for you. Consider how you write best, then test your assumptions. This will go a long way to making you the best writer you can possibly be.

WHAT ARE YOU READING?

Before we look at using these precious words to improve our writing, let me ask you one very important question: What did you read last night? I want to know what's sitting on your bedside table with a bookmark sticking out of it. Yes—a good old-fashioned book! Go searching for advice on how to write better and the first thing you'll find will be to read. Stephen King will tell you: "If you don't have the time to read, you don't have the time (or tools) to write. Simple as that." And some are even as blunt as to claim that if you don't read, you can't possibly write. This applies to everyone. Even if your field is advanced quantum mechanics, you can still learn from the travel writing of Paul Theroux, the science fiction of Octavia Butler, or the poetry of Anna Akhmatova.

So what did you read last night? If the answer is nothing (and I include social media as "nothing"), you get no points and a seriously disapproving look from me. If you read news of some sort, you'll get 50 percent—that's 25 percent for reading and 25 percent for staying abreast of what's happening in the world (another area where academics traditionally score very badly). But to get full marks, you need to be reading something that is completely unrelated to your work or area of expertise. Why?

Well, your brain is like a sponge. It is where we store the words, metaphors, idioms, and imagery that we need to communicate, and it has a limitless capacity. It really is an amazing thing. Throughout the day, you take in a huge number of words from your chosen field. Every email you read, every report you refer to, every phone call you make can potentially add more words to your vocabulary. But these are all "work" words. If you are an astrophysicist, for example, the chances are your brain is chock-full of all the astrophysics words you could ever need. But the rest of us don't speak astrophysics. This means you need different words to communicate to us, the sorts of words that we can understand. So how do you acquire these words? The answer is simple: you read crime, poetry, romance, play scripts, gardening books, biographies...anything! The wider and more varied your reading is, the better your chances of expanding your vocabulary and acquiring new and exciting ways of expressing yourself.

• • •

Better writing always starts with clarity of thought and ideas. If you're not crystal clear about what you want to say right from the start, by the time your message gets to its intended recipient, it can be seriously distorted and sometimes nothing like your original intentions. So let's have a look at what you've got to say.

4

WHAT DO YOU HAVE TO SAY?

You know a lot. Quite a lot. But not everything
you know is of interest to your audience.
So let's start sifting and sorting.

I am sure you've worked this out by now, but as an academic, you are never going to have enough space to be able to say or write everything you want to. Even with the luxury of eighty thousand or ninety thousand words in a PhD thesis, for example, you still have to leave an awful lot out. You are constantly sifting and sorting—considering each fact, each bit of data, each anecdote, and including it or discarding it. And when you are communicating to audiences outside academia, your word limits and time restrictions are going to be much smaller than anything you've ever encountered before.

So how do you know what to leave in, what to say?

LOOKING FOR STORIES

Try treating the task at hand in the same way you'd approach having a cup of coffee with someone. When you sit and chat with someone, you tell them what you think they might like to hear, don't you?

You filter all the things you could possibly say until you are left with the parts that your coffee date might find interesting. You gauge their reaction and tweak your content as you go along. But essentially, you're talking *to* them and *for* them. You're not saying things just for the sake of it, and you're certainly not talking to hear the sound of your own voice. And of course, there's also the other half of what makes for good conversation—listening. Really, the key to successfully engaging with any audience is to remember it's always a dialogue.

Translating this to writing and speaking about your research to the outside world means thinking about what your audience would like to hear about, what they might find interesting and relevant. Which makes defining your audience all the more important. You can't tailor your content for an audience you don't know. But more on that soon.

Think of this part of the process as strip-mining your research for stories. And when I say stories, I mean the experiments, the data, and the world-changing outcomes, but also the journey you took to get there and the characters you met along the way. Your work is like a huge rock face, and you need to be on the lookout for those seams of gold hidden within it that bring your work to life in an exciting and accessible way. This sorting process is actually not as hard as you might think, particularly if you approach it from a reductive rather than an additive way. Strip away your research to expose the stories within, and always adopt a ruthless attitude. Look at everything you could possibly include in your story or blog post or tweet, and assume you are going to delete it. Your default position should be: *This couldn't possibly be of interest to anyone. It must go!* And then challenge that statement. If you can persuade yourself that your audience might actually want to hear this little morsel, this fascinating fact, this particular story, then you are allowed to leave it in. But don't allow yourself to be a pushover! Make sure your argument is very convincing.

You are probably going to need several attempts at this process—always cutting back, paring the story to its core until you arrive not only at the desired word length but also at the sort of content that will keep your audience reading right until the end. A good rule of thumb is that every lesson in your story should be able to be reduced to a one-line bullet point. If you can summarize your five-hundred-word story in, say, ten single-line bullet points, you've probably got the skeleton of an interesting read.

And it probably won't come as a surprise that the general public is very interested in outcomes and results. If you have achieved something groundbreaking, don't hold back—tell us that up front and you'll have us hooked. NASA is very good at this. Of course it helps to have a huge budget and a whole department devoted to getting the word out, but when the *Curiosity* rover found organic matter in Martian soil a couple of years back, it hit the front pages within hours of the results being in.

Now you may be making these decisions for a blog post or a tweet, so the process might be quite quick. But you might also have to do this for an article, a chapter, or even a book. We're talking potentially tens of thousands of words and months of your time here. How do you maintain the momentum and concentration when the sorting process is that extended?

Australian historian Robyn Annear gave my favorite answer to that question. Robyn is as much a collector as she is a researcher—she often begins by surrounding herself with enough content to fill a whole series of books rather than the single volume her publisher is expecting her to write. When she was talking to my students, she was doing the research for a history of the wrecking company that spent most of the twentieth century transforming Melbourne's skyline. As always, the reports, data, and anecdotes were beginning to build up. So what did she do? She wrote herself a mission statement for the book: "In this book, I will..." She printed it out and stuck it above her computer so it was impossible to ignore. Then, whenever the question of whether or not something belonged in the book came up, the answer was there for her. I think it's a brilliant trick and well worth using.

WHAT ARE READERS INTERESTED IN?

Of course, no piece of writing, no story ever lives in isolation. As an expert, you will often find yourself writing different versions of similar stories. Sometimes you're telling the same story for a different audience or a different publication, and sometimes you are continuing or enlarging on a story for the same audience in the same publication. These overlaps and crossovers will help you refine your understanding of what your audience is interested in. This is particularly true in the digital world—if you write for *The Conversation*, for example—where you can see exactly how many people have accessed your writing and whether they have read all of it or just moved on after the first paragraph. You can also see how they found your work in the first place. Was it from a link on a colleague's blog? Through a search engine? Even the simplest analysis of reading patterns will give you some very significant data to help you refine your writing.

Of real relevance here is how newspapers now use analytics to determine much of their content. These days, newspapers look at the data they get from their online readerships and use that to focus on subject areas that their readers find interesting and keep coming back to. They also use this information when choosing freelance writers to contribute to their pages. If you are lucky enough to repeatedly get high numbers of readers looking at your writing, you may find yourself being invited and even commissioned to contribute to the pages of that publication. And having high numbers of social media followers in your own right will keep you firmly at the front of the commissioning editor's mind. While all this is a very commercially minded approach to the whole sifting-and-sorting question, it really isn't that far removed from what you need to be doing to ensure you are giving your audiences what they want to read and hear.

5

WHO ARE YOU TALKING TO?

Writing well is a brilliant thing—certainly something we all need to do—but if you don't know who you're writing for, it can be a bit of a wasted effort.

Your audience determines absolutely everything about the way you write. Essentially you must write in a way that they can understand, in the language they are used to. What sort of language should you use? How complex should it be? How formal or informal? What cultural reference points can you include? These are just a few of the ways in which you must accommodate your audience's needs. If you get these things right, your writing can't help but be better and more effective.

You're going to be hearing a lot about my favorite ratio—49:51. In this instance, it represents the fact that your audience is at least 51 percent of the process. That means that you, the communicator, are—at the very most—49 percent of the equation. Let's face it, unless your work is intended only for an old-fashioned diary with a lock and key, someone else is always going to consume your words; you are *never* writing for yourself. Nowhere is this clearer than in the situation where you meet a colleague who has been off somewhere giving a spectacularly unsuccessful talk. "They just didn't get it!" they will cry out in frustration. They might think they are apportioning blame to a disappointingly unintelligent audience. In fact, as far as I am concerned, they are admitting failure.

It is never the audience's job to "get it." It is your job to make sure they get it. I say again: **your audience matters more than you do.** And the key to ensuring they get it each and every time is to know exactly who they are.

THE "LAY" AUDIENCE

And while we are talking about your audience, let's have a quick look at what I call "the myth of the lay audience." As an academic, you'll often hear about writing for a "lay" or "general" audience. Usually, this will simply clarify that you are writing for a nonacademic audience or publication, but quite often it also comes with a certain tone—a bit of an attitude that suggests it's only a lay audience, so you needn't make much effort. The reality is that there is no such thing as this mythical lay audience. Your audience can be, and often is, anyone around you. We are all both experts and lay audience members depending on the area of expertise under discussion. So if you write for or speak to an audience on the basis that they are your equals—they are just as smart, intelligent, well connected as you—but they just haven't done the same research as you, you will be fine. Just treat them with respect.

But if you decide to ignore all this advice and "dumb it down"—to use another horrible phrase—because it's just a lay audience, it will only end badly. Any audience knows when they are being patronized or condescended to. And without exception, they hate it. That, in itself, is bad enough, but when you are writing for a nonacademic audience, you have the added factor that your audience is under no obligation to read your work. Unlike your peers and colleagues in academia who are reviewing, assessing, or examining what you have to say, we the general public are reading your work because we want to. And if we don't want to, we stop reading. It's as simple as that. And guess what is one of the easiest ways to stop us reading? That's right: dumbing down. The moment we feel you are talking down to us, we put down the paper, we close the book, and we walk away.

HOW IMPORTANT IS THE AUDIENCE?

You need to start with the mindset that all writing is a two-way form of communication. You and your reader are having a conversation or a dialogue. It doesn't matter that you are on opposite sides of the planet and will probably never meet. See the reader in your mind as you write, and write *for them*.

The golden rule of communication is that when we communicate, we are always doing it for someone else. With the sole exception of the aforementioned diary hidden under the mattress away from the prying eyes of little brothers, every piece of writing you put together, every speech you make is for someone else. And that someone else matters more than you.

WHO ARE YOUR READERS?

One of the first things I have students do is think about who their readers might be. Some get this straightaway and quickly work out who their niche audiences are. Some have a less realistic version of this—"I am writing a cultural and social history of the motor vehicle in Melbourne, Australia, over the hundred years leading up to 1972, so my audience is anyone in the world who drives a car." (And no, I didn't make that up. I wish I had.) And some just see their readership as "the general public," which simply does not exist—certainly not as a discrete, defined readership. In fact, there is an infinite number of niche audiences, as many as there are topics for them to be interested in. Your job is to identify them, find them, and target them.

Of course, as with greatness, occasionally writers will find their readers thrust upon 'em. Microbiologist and popular science writer Idan Ben-Barak took a perfectly delightful look at the wonderful world of microbes in *Small Wonders*. What he didn't anticipate was the fact that his very dry sense of humor coupled with the general ickiness of bacteria would be a magnet for teenage boys and would win him the 2010 American Association for the Advancement of Science/Subaru Science Books and Films Prize for Excellence in Science Books in...wait for it...the Young Adult category. Anything to get boys reading, I say!

So how do we find our audiences? The answer is quite simple. Start by taking a look in the mirror. You and your peers, colleagues, and even interested friends are good examples of your own audiences. You are, after all, interested in what you do. Where do you go to find your information? What news outlets do you access? Do you read old-fashioned ink on paper, or do you go online? Do you stream, download, or wait for free-to-air TV? Do you listen to podcasts as you cook, jog, or walk the dog, or do you tune in to the radio to see what's on?

What you need to do is to profile yourself and a few of your colleagues and friends and build up a picture of your "typical" audience member. You want a few simple demographics and a bit of a listening/watching/reading pattern. This becomes your benchmark and will tell you where to start. Of course, you want to eventually build on this audience, but you can't do that without establishing some sort of a benchmark. And like you, your audience will grow and develop and change, so you need to be constantly recalibrating your understanding of them.

I know many, many writers who put a photo of their archetypical reader up next to their computer. Sometimes it's someone they know; sometimes it's just a photo cut out of a magazine. They might give this hypothetical reader a name. This familiar face acts as a constant reminder that you are writing for someone else and that you need to come up with the goods for them, not for you.

Another useful trick is to look for people like you. As much as you are a unique individual, there will be people working in similar areas and writing and speaking about similar or related topics. Who are their audiences? Who are they writing and speaking to? While you are not going to steal their audiences, you can take a good, hard look at them to see the type of people they are.

Now, far be it from me to encourage exploitation in the classroom, but for those of you with teaching positions, never forget that your students are a valuable resource for you as a writer and communicator. They can quite easily function as first readers, a beta test group, or a sounding board to road test your work.

GROWING YOUR AUDIENCE

Once you have established a bit of a baseline for your core audience, think about growing it. When you give a talk in the community or appear on a panel at a conference, for example, always keep your eye on the audience. What sort of people have turned up to find out about the topic you are talking on? Be particularly attentive at question time—that's often when you can really get to know your audience. If you are on talk radio, who calls in to ask questions? Again, this is a great way to really get to know your audience.

But then you also need to factor in a wider range of interests on the part of your audience. Yes, they are interested in your blog because of your groundbreaking work on cloning, let's say, but while you are focused in an almost obsessive way on this topic, your audience may also be interested in the wider world of genetics, animals, agriculture, science, nature, and the environment. And if they are interested in your work and also interested in these topics, they will in all probability be interested in what you have to say about these areas too.

The other element worth considering is what has brought your audience to you, whether that's as an audience member at a talk or as a reader of your writing. An interesting approach is to treat each potential audience member as someone who has a question or a challenge or a problem—possibly one that they may not even know they have if they're just browsing—that you as an expert can help them with. If you can think a bit laterally—creatively even—then come up with what this might be and address it, you are well on the way to winning them over.

6

FINDING THE RIGHT FORM

Once you know what you want to say and who you're talking to, then you need to decide how to talk to them. Or, more accurately, where to talk to them.

Once you decide to talk to the world outside the academy, you have more than a few choices of platforms where you can engage with interested audiences. What is really interesting is how different these audiences can be, even when looking at quite similar channels for communication.

One of the first people I came across who really knew how to exploit the digital world was Associate Professor Meredith Nash, a sociologist from the University of Tasmania, who created the Baby Bump Project. This was back in 2005 when the rest of academia was still thinking about possibly setting up a website at some point in the future. Meredith was already a prolific and wide-ranging contributor to the online conversation: she had words on her Facebook page, blog, and website; images on Flickr and Tumblr; and video on YouTube and Vimeo. When she was at the University of Melbourne, Meredith presented to workshops, and she would tell them that each channel had its own, quite discrete audience. She had followers who would read short bursts on their phones on the way to work, others who would sit down at their desks and read longer pieces on their laptops, and some who would even wait until the evening to sit down and watch a video or listen to a podcast. And surprisingly, Meredith had found that these groups were quite distinct, with nowhere near as much overlap between them as you'd expect. Current practice in what is now called digital asset management shows this is still true, and analysts have identified factors like location or time of day or user activity (whether at work or at home, for example) as influencing which channel a user will turn to at any given time.

You are probably going to start with one or two ways of sharing your thoughts and discoveries with the world, so it's important to choose the right ways. Start by looking at yourself, your peers, your friends, and your colleagues. Pose yourself a few questions, and try the same questions on your friends—treat them as a bit of a focus group, if you like. Ask yourself: Where should I go to find out about my research topics outside the normal academic channels I use? Or, alternatively, if you weren't researching your topic but wanted to find out about it, where would you go to find information on it? And if you're not sure about the answer, try it. It only takes a few seconds, and sometimes Google can be your friend.

Topicality will often influence this—some subjects are "newsier," whereas others might have a more timeless or ongoing relevance. Newsworthy subject matter will obviously be found in places like online news sites or in some of the faster, more immediate channels like Twitter, whereas other topics might take you to more specialized and niche parts of the internet.

The more time you put into this exercise—building on the

previous exercises profiling your audiences and their interests—the more detailed the results you will generate and the more strategic you will be about spreading the word. But it is important that you do some of this planning; otherwise, you risk simply stabbing in the dark and only ever hitting your target (or in all likelihood not hitting it) through sheer luck.

Given that you will probably find that you have more than one topic you can write about, more than a few different niche audiences you can talk to, and a variety of places those audiences go to find their information, it could be useful to create a matrix to guide you along the way. A simple Excel spreadsheet will do. One axis should show your subject headings, the other the audiences who might want to hear about them, and where the axes intersect the forums where that communication could take place. You might try this with short pieces for some of the sites you subscribe to, then maybe pitch an explainer on your topic to The Conversation, and then build up to something a little more mainstream like your local public broadcaster. But make sure your matrix is flexible. Like all plans, it will only be of use if it is a living document that is responsive to change and the influence of external factors and is constantly kept up-to-date.

And now that you have a plan to guide you with sharing your research with the world, let's look at the voice—the quintessential written essence of you—that your readers are going to meet when they look at the pages you have written.

7

FINDING YOUR VOICE

In this conversation that you and your reader are
having, it's now time to express your personality
and to put something of yourself on the page.
It's time to find your "writer's voice."

Sharing your research with the outside world in newspapers,
magazines, and online is a very different process from publishing journal articles or making conference presentations,
and one of the big, key differences is how much of you is there in
the process. In academia, you'll often hear the phrase *getting the data
out there*. It's a very impersonal process where you are not so much
encouraged as instructed to step right out of the picture and let the
results speak for themselves. This is how it should be. But not when
we are talking to the rest of the world.

Your outside audiences are as interested in you as they are in the
incredible discoveries you have made. They love the process; they
are interested in you as a person and like to get an idea in their heads
of you at work. I often say that while we love Tutankhamun, his
sarcophagus, and his death mask, we also love the story of Howard
Carter removing that brick and shining a light into the hole. I am

sure you've heard it before: "For the moment—an eternity it must have seemed to the others standing by—I was struck dumb with amazement, and when Lord Carnarvon, unable to stand in suspense any longer, inquired anxiously, 'Can you see anything?,' it was all I could do to get out the words 'Yes, wonderful things!'" It's hard not to get excited by that, isn't it?

So how do you put yourself in the story? To begin, be yourself; just talk to us like you would to any other human being over a coffee. You're going to "wear your knowledge lightly," as I heard it perfectly expressed once. You're just going to chat.

Your writer's voice is the essence of you on the page. It's what makes your writing yours and yours alone. Remember—this is your story. No one else knows what you do or cares about it like you do. It would be odd to express that passion in anything other than your own voice.

Bill Bryson is a good example of the writer's voice. Among other things, Bill writes very funny travel books with a gentle, self-deprecating sense of humor and a wry tone that is both highly sophisticated and slightly naive at the same time. He's a great writer. If ever you see him speak or listen to his audiobooks, his unique voice will stick in your head forever. And from then on, you'll always hear that voice when you read his work. In fact, if you were a fan and I were to hand you a piece of unattributed travel writing about a place you didn't know he had visited and it had the same tone, sense of humor, and sensibilities, a little voice in your head would say, "This sounds exactly like Bill Bryson." And that's how a good writer's voice works.

All you can really do to develop your writer's voice is write more and watch it flourish and grow all on its own, organically and at its own pace. But to nurture it, there are three particularly effective things you can do.

First, just be a little self-aware. If you want to stamp your personality on your writing, you probably need to at least have some idea of what that personality is. What are you like? Are you in awe of the world and the human race or highly cynical of people in general? Are you serious, or do you prefer a light touch and a sprinkling of humor? I am a big fan of using your imagination and envisioning, or even self-fulfilling prophecies. Fast-forward in your mind a few years to the time when you are a successful nonfiction writer appearing at events around the world. What does that future you sound like when they are being interviewed? Because that's the person who your readers will also want to meet on the page.

Second comes reading. Reading is generally the key to doing everything better for a serious writer, but I think observing other writers at work, hearing their voices, and analyzing what makes them distinct and memorable will really help you achieve the same effect with your words. Again, nothing too deep is required—just a wide reading of as many and as varied a bunch of writers as you can think of.

And third, reading goes hand in hand with reading aloud. Print out a page or two of your writing, and find yourself a quiet spot where you can read out loud quite unselfconsciously. Again, use your imagination. Maybe a publisher has asked you to do the audiobook of your work. How will it sound? What do you like about the way that you sound? And more importantly, what do you not like that you would like to change?

Of course the content and, to a lesser extent, the form are going to dictate how much of yourself ends up on the page. A highly personal opinion piece should sound...well...highly personal, whereas something more factual can be a little more restrained.

But it's hugely important that you have fun when writing. While it can be a hard slog to get a writing assignment finished, essentially you should enjoy the process. Because if you don't, it will show. And if you don't enjoy writing something, do you think we are going to enjoy reading it? Probably not. Your writer's voice should contain and communicate the joy and passion you have for your topic and your writing. If it's any good, it will bring your readers back to your work again and again and again.

8

THE PRACTICALITIES

Now let's get down to practicalities: how to write about complex, specialist subjects for a nonspecialist, nonacademic, but still smart readership.

I t's very important that you organize your thoughts before writing. Unlike writing fiction, writing nonfiction is not a journey of discovery. Even if you are working through the answers to a research question, that question and the way you intend to answer it need to be worked out in advance. Sitting in front of your keyboard waiting for the muse to strike is at best optimistic and, in all likelihood, probably a complete waste of your time. In fact, you can pretty much guarantee that the muse will always be noticeably absent at the time you need them the most.

Which is why you need to rely on the Nike principle and "just do it." You never see an Olympic rowing team standing by the water waiting until they are in the mood to go fast; they get in there day after day and just row. Eventually, through sheer persistence and hard work, they will go faster. Your writing is no different from that. In fact, I'd venture that writing is more like training or exercise than you realize; if you set a regular schedule or routine and write every day, your writing "muscle" cannot help but get stronger. Do the odd bit of writing here and there when you feel in the mood, and your writing muscle will remain flabby and eventually wither.

BE BRIEF

First, and possibly most importantly, think short. We are looking for short words in short sentences in shorter paragraphs. And if you're writing a book, we are expecting short chapters in a short book. I heard a wonderful story about a publisher who was looking for new manuscripts in which each chapter was two subway stops long—about four minutes of reading time.

BE ACTIVE

Always choose active verbs over passive verbs: "I think," not "it is thought"; "I consider," not "it is considered"; "I suggest," not "it is suggested." We are genuinely interested in you and your research, so be honest and tell us what you think. The impersonal "it is thought" is tantamount to linguistic cowardice on this score, whereas a simple little pronoun like "I" puts you front and center in the picture. And of course, if you are not doing the thinking in the "it is thought," that's even more confusing, as the audience tries to work out who on earth you're talking about.

When you hide behind the language with something like "it is often suggested that," all you do is raise questions in your audience's mind. Your aim as a communicator is 100 percent of your audience's attention 100 percent of the time—and nothing less. If you say "it is often suggested that" and leave your listener or reader wondering who did the suggesting and when the suggesting might have happened and what the circumstances of the suggesting were, then they are not giving you their full attention. And if they are not giving you their full attention, you have failed as a communicator. Here's a silly example just to really make the point. Imagine you are a scientist and you announce, "I have cured cancer." Your audience would gasp "You have?!" Then imagine making the same announcement using the passive voice: "Cancer has been cured by me." You'll have a very confused audience scratching their heads and asking, "What did he say?"

BE CLEAR

Try to avoid jargon or acronyms; universities love these, but no one else does. I spend my days trying to decipher emails about a meeting between the PVC and the DVC at the CEC and often just give up and press the Delete button. Seriously. And I don't want to hear about postcolonial neologisms or ontological discourse. Stay well away from these kinds of "academic" words, even though your research is probably full of them. Quite simply, you are communicating with an audience, and you should do so in the language that your audience speaks. If they are not fluent in Esperanto, don't use it, and if they don't speak Jargonese or Acronymic, then neither should you.

If you're really not sure what jargon is—and I admit, when you are totally immersed in a topic and only talk about it to people who are equally immersed, it's easy to lose sight of what is and isn't jargon—imagine being asked to give an impromptu talk to another faculty on the other side of campus. How would you describe your research to people from a completely different field? And if you still don't understand how off-putting jargon can be to an outsider, go to a café on a Sunday morning, sit next to a group of sweaty middle-aged men in Lycra, and listen to them talk about the criterium or the peloton.

For similar reasons, always qualify any unknowns such as concepts, people, places, or institutions. The golden rule here is that if there is even the tiniest possibility of one member of your audience not knowing about something you are discussing, then you need to qualify it. Don't just name-drop the most significant researcher in your field—let's call her Professor Daiso Watanabe—but tell us who she is and what she's done: Professor Daiso Watanabe, the person who discovered the lost temple of whatever it was she discovered. And then you're good to go.

While we're on Professor Watanabe, let me just tick off another bugbear of mine—she can be Professor Daiso Watanabe, she can be Daiso Watanabe, she can even be Daiso if you know her well, but please don't do that academic surname thing where she is just reduced to "Watanabe." It just sounds horrible, patronizing, and disrespectful.

I had to bite my tongue the other day when someone started to answer a perfectly simple question with the phrase *hierarchies of transitory knowledge*. If you are going to use language like that when talking to audiences outside academia, it's probably more efficient to get a T-shirt made that says "I am a wanker." You'll be sending the same message.

And while we're on the subject, the line about the T-shirt boasting "I am a wanker" is a good example of the surprisingly frequent insularity of the English language, as I found out the first time I used it in front of an audience in Vancouver, only to be faced by blank, uncomprehending faces. I sometimes wonder if I'm the only lecturer on the planet to have fielded the question, "Excuse me, but what is a wanker?'

Watch out for those tricky words that mean one thing on Planet Academia and another on Planet Earth. Pity the poor scientist who bursts out of the lab door in a "Eureka!" moment shouting "I've got a theory!" only to be confronted by the general public, who counter with "Yes, but it's only a theory."

MAKE EVERY WORD COUNT

Make sure every word you write and every sentence you use is doing something. We really don't have room for passengers in our writing.

There's a great essay by George Orwell—"Politics and the English Language"—written in 1946. Orwell was probably one of the most efficient writers ever to write in English—there are very few words on his pages that aren't working to maximum effect. He was constantly questioning himself and suggested that any writer worth their salt should ask themselves four questions every time their pen was poised above the blank page:

1. What am I trying to say?
2. What words will express it?
3. What image or idiom will make it clearer?
4. Is this image fresh enough to have an effect?

Follow that advice, make every word you use justify its existence, and you will be a writer to be reckoned with.

Pare your writing back to the absolute essentials, remove all redundancies, and don't repeat yourself. Don't repeat yourself. Don't repeat yourself. An old joke, I know, but a serious point. There is a bit of a tradition in academia, often called "telegraphing" or "sign-posting," of telling us what you are about to say, then actually telling us, and finally telling us what you have just told us. To my mind, two of those are entirely redundant.

Think about your writing in terms of distillation and crystallization. In practical terms, this means that if you want to write a thousand-word piece, the very first thing you do is dash off (and I do really mean dash off) a two-thousand-word piece, then much more slowly and painstakingly edit it down. By the time you are left with one thousand words, every single word on your page will have survived a culling process and be actually doing something. Your writing will have no passengers and no freeloaders. It's a bit like creating a reduction or a jus in cooking terms—I am sure you know exactly what I am talking about from all those expensive French dinners your massive academic salaries have made affordable to you. No? OK, you've seen *MasterChef*, right? Big white plate, seven peas on the left, half a potato up top, minuscule piece of meat hiding down at the bottom, and a smear of brown stuff across the middle? The brown stuff started life as a liter of stock and a liter of red wine and all sorts of other bits and pieces but ended up barely filling a teaspoon while still containing all the depth, flavor, and complexity of the original contents. Your writing should be exactly like this—short, sharp, and to the point, but containing all the information, complexity, and nuance of all the extraneous words you have cut out along the way.

TRY LITERARY DEVICES

When you are writing about your research for your new, non-academic audiences, you can also start to employ a much wider range of literary devices and effects than you are currently used to relying on in your academic writing. In fact, I'd like you to soak up some of the influences of the fiction I think you should be reading and start to experiment with

- creativity, imagination, and emotion;
- imagery, metaphors, and figures of speech;
- pacing, structure, and narrative arcs;
- voice, three-dimensional characters, and dialogue; and
- action and excitement.

I think it's also a good idea to try to make your writing invisible. Put simply: if your readers are looking at your writing, they're not reading its content, are they? Your writing shouldn't draw attention to itself; it should be natural, relaxed, and almost conversational, but never showy. After all, your writing is only the vehicle to allow the ideas it is conveying to shine through. It's always nice if someone says that your writing is good, but it's even nicer if they say that *after* remarking on your amazing discoveries. Mostly, this can be achieved by ensuring every word you use is there for a reason. Anything on the page that can't justify its existence is simply window dressing.

READ IT ALOUD

And my last piece of advice on how to write better? Read out loud to yourself. Sometimes the simplest ideas are the best. Just try it; read something to yourself in your head, and your eyes, which are forgiving and lazy, will tell you that it looks fine, that it's really good, maybe even that it's brilliant. Then read it out loud, and let your ears take over. Your ears are much more critical and piercingly unforgiving. Suddenly the writing your eyes told you was brilliant seems—or sounds—very lackluster indeed.

• • •

As a general rule, I think any time spent reading how-to-write books or attending how-to-write courses is time that could be better spent writing, but I do make the odd exception to that rule. One is a piece that first appeared in *Business Insider* in 2015 called "22 Lessons from Stephen King on How to Be a Great Writer." It's exactly what the title suggests, with the lessons all taken from Mr. King's book *On Writing*. Go find the article and take a look; it won't take much of your valuable writing time, but it will leave you inspired and motivated. And whether you like his writing or not, Mr. King certainly knows how to move a few units, as they say in publishing. Let's just hope you don't need Lesson 14—"Realize that you don't need drugs to be a good writer!"

9

LESS IS MORE— THE ALL-IMPORTANT ART OF EDITING

Getting rid of padding, fill, fluff, and waffle and making sure you only use as many words as you need. And, of course, killing your darlings—let's not forget that.

I am sure you did some sort of rudimentary editing of your own work at school. You would have looked at the editing process in its simplest form and considered things like spelling, capitalization, punctuation, grammar, sentence structure, subject-verb agreement, consistent verb tense, and word usage. If you didn't do any of this at school, there are plenty of books and websites that will set you straight (a few are listed at the back of this book). At that level, editing is not hard. But real editing is so much more than that.

I am talking about you editing your own work here. Of course, it's entirely possible to have someone else edit your work, and if you get to write a book for a commercial publisher, you'll be lucky enough to work with an editor, but freelance editors cost money—sometimes quite a bit of money. That's because they are good and can—and more often than not *do*—work miracles. Truman Capote got it right: "I'm all for the scissors. I believe more in the scissors than I do in the pencil." So for now, we're going to edit our own work.

Editing is actually the most important part of the writing process. Remember the ratio 49:51? In this case, editing is, as far as I am concerned, at least 51 percent of the process, while writing is at the very most 49 percent. I remember seeing a *Guardian* interview with the extraordinarily creative and often out-of-left-field British writer Will Self where he encouraged writers to keep writing without looking back. Then, he wrote, "you have a substantial body of work before you get down to the real work...the edit." Now, editing does look at the nitty-gritty details of your writing, the sort of stuff you did at school, but it starts way before that with the big, overall picture. It's here that you pick up things that you don't notice when you are writing because you are just too close, and it's where you shape your story, making it readable and engaging. But editing is also where you take on the role of business manager for your writing. Whether you are being paid to write or not, whoever you are submitting your work to will want it formatted and submitted in a particular way. This is all part of the editing process.

You can think of editing as a bit like looking at your work through a microscope or a zoom lens. It starts wide with the overall structure; then it zooms in a bit closer to examine the structure within each of your paragraphs; then closer still, with the structure and effectiveness of individual sentences within the paragraphs; then it looks at individual words and, lastly, punctuation. After that, you take a step backward to look at the bigger picture again, but this time with an eye to overall clarity and meaning. Is the piece doing what it is supposed to do—convincing us, enthralling us, informing us? Then finally, you take another look at the overall piece, this time concentrating on style and "spine"—the glue that holds all the various elements together to form a single cohesive piece of writing. How well written is the piece? Does it follow the rules of whichever genre it is operating in?

Of course, editing is not just about looking—that's just the beginning. The editing process is actually much more about rewriting.

It's probably worth just touching on one thing at this point—the difference between editing and proofreading, as these terms are often used interchangeably and incorrectly. Just to be clear: editing is a long and many-layered process that you start as soon as you've finished your first draft. It begins with the big picture—the structure and how all the elements hold together—and ends up at all the commas, semicolons, and full stops. Proofreading is the final stage of that process when you read very closely and focus on such errors as misspellings and mistakes in grammar and punctuation. Proofreading only happens *after* you have finished all the other parts of the editing process.

Some people have alpha and beta testing as part of their editorial process. This is entirely up to you. I tend not to, but then my report card always used to say "doesn't play well with others." I know writers who have individuals and groups they share their work with, seeking constructive comments and honest feedback. Your choice, but perhaps bear in mind Margaret Atwood's very sage advice not to share your work with anyone with whom you are currently romantically involved...unless, of course, you don't mind ending that relationship.

WRITER VS. EDITOR

While editing is a very involved and complex process requiring a particular skill set, British writer Zadie Smith captures it perfectly: "The secret to editing your work is simple: you need to become its reader instead of its writer."

When you edit your own work, you have to become two very different people. First, you have to be a writer. Writers are subjective, emotional, passionate, personal, and attached, and their writing comes from the heart.

Now you need to take on a second personality. You have to be an editor. Editors are objective, clinical, dispassionate, impersonal, and detached, and their approach to their work comes from the mind.

You need to develop both of these very different personalities; there's you, the writer, who is a warm and fuzzy, feeling and caring kind of person who writes from the heart. And there's you, the editor, who is obsessive, even a little bit anal, and who works from the brain. And you need to be able to switch from writer to editor for every piece of writing you do. Actually, that's not as hard as it sounds, and like everything in life, it gets a whole lot easier if you practice it.

WHEN TO EDIT

Before we work out *how* to edit, I think I should probably tell you *when* to edit. I cannot emphasize this enough: you edit *when you have finished writing*. Not before. Never before. Sure, you can fiddle around with punctuation and spelling and the odd bit of grammar along the way, but you can't take a look at that amazing closing paragraph you've just poured your heart and soul into and say, "Hang on; that would make an even more powerful opening statement to hook the reader in." As we've seen, editing is a holistic thing. It looks at the structure of the writing, the flow of ideas, the story arc (which applies to nonfiction too), and the development of the narrative or argument. None of these can possibly be changed until the whole piece is finished. And if you are going to be changing between your writing hat and your editing hat, it makes much more sense to do it once for each piece of writing rather than to keep doing it repeatedly again and again and again. That way lies madness!

Editing is also so much more effective if you can put some distance—both physical and chronological—between the writing and the editing process. When you finish writing, close the laptop or put the pen down and walk away from your work—if your budget permits, for a week or two. Anything you can do to give you a sense of detachment from your writing will make the next stage of the process so much easier. Ideally, when you return to the work and put your editor's hat on, the writing should seem new and unfamiliar.

Self-awareness is a wonderful thing. We all make mistakes when we write—we wouldn't be human if we didn't—but luckily, we tend to make the same mistakes over and over again. So if we become aware of our own bad habits, we should be able to see them coming and, if not eliminate them, at least anticipate them and head them off at the pass, so to speak.

HOW LONG SHOULD YOU EDIT FOR?

How much time you spend editing is crucial. I seriously think you should edit for at least as long as you write. Ideally more. Editing should never be an afterthought or a quick tidying up that happens when you hit the deadline or someone demands that you submit. If I set a one-hour writing exercise in class, I can always spot the really committed writers in the group—they are the ones who will glance at their watches around the thirty-minute mark, pick up their metaphorical red pens, and start editing.

And just in case you think you are that rare beast, the writer who can knock off a perfect final draft in one go, let me explain something: you aren't. No matter how good you are, expect to write many, many drafts. In fact, I tend to think that the writing process is a finite process—you instinctively know when you've got nothing more to say. Editing, on the other hand, is infinite—you can always do just that little bit more. In many ways, you are like a sculptor with a huge block of stone or wood; there's always a little bit more that can be shaved off to make the surface smoother.

As an academic, you have an added degree of difficulty with your writing that, in editing, you need to be constantly on the lookout for. You hedge. You know what I mean: you suggest that something may possibly appear to be so; at least, perhaps it is. But that's not how the rest of us talk. So be confident, and be certain. And don't worry—we know that science changes, research discovers new things, and sometimes you have to revise your conclusions. We just want to hear you express a strong opinion based on what you know at the time.

HOW TO EDIT...WELL

So how do we edit? Or, more importantly, how do we edit *well*? Over the years, after hearing hundreds of writers answer the question "What's the best way to edit?" I have amassed quite a good list of how-to techniques. I must have heard of every possible way under the sun that you can edit your writing, but interestingly there are five tried-and-tested methods that come up again and again. So here they are: the "greatest hits" of editing.

One Word at a Time

What this technique aims to do is detach you from your writing. And it really is very, very simple. All you have to do is read your work slowly...one...word...at...a...time. How do you make yourself do this? Easy—by getting a ruler, a red pen, or a highlighter and underlining, circling, or highlighting every single word...one...word...at...a...time. If you read the words out loud as you do this, so much the better. That will slow you down even more. And if you do this, it is impossible to become lost in your own beautiful writing and so much easier to be analytical and critical. You can even read syllables, not words. (This is e-ven slow-er. Much, much slow-er.)

Best Sentence Bypass

I've also heard this described as the *worst sentence bypass* and even with *paragraph* substituted for *sentence*. It's a very simple process. First, print out the piece of writing you want to edit—and apologies to the trees here, but just about every writer I've talked to has said that editing is always better done on paper, not onscreen—then read it a few times and decide which sentence is your very best sentence: the one you sweated blood and tears over, the one that kept you up all night, the one that will win you the Pulitzer Prize. Found it? Good! Now cut it out. And unless you can really—and I mean really—justify putting it back in, leave it out. Your default position should be to delete.

Your aim is to have every sentence on the page achieving something. Whether it's advancing a narrative, explaining a technique, or developing a character doesn't matter, but it should be doing something. If it isn't, you don't need it. So you start with a piece that's, let's say, one hundred sentences long, you find the best one, delete it, see that it was actually doing nothing other than standing around looking pretty, and leave it out. This leaves you with a ninety-nine-sentence piece. What do you do then? You do it all over again. Find what was the second-best sentence, which has now been promoted to the best-sentence spot, and delete that one. See if its removal has affected your writing in any way. If it hasn't, leave it out. And keep on doing this. You might find that your one-hundred-sentence piece ends up only fifty sentences long, but you know that every single word on that page is there for a reason. And your readers will thank you for it! If you need a bit of a safety net here—or if you are involved in a collaboration—you can always track your changes, but I still want you to be absolutely ruthless. Show no mercy!

Bit by Bit Backward

This is another technique designed to prevent you from being seduced by your own writing. Start with the very last line, and read it as critically as you can. Fix it, delete it, do whatever needs doing. Then read and deal with the penultimate line. Then the antepenultimate line. And so on. Just read backward. It's a bit like reading a crime or mystery book and being told right at the start that it was the butler whodunit. You're not going to read the rest of the book wondering who the murderer is, are you? It's another amazingly simple way to ensure a detached and critical approach to your work.

Slash and Burn

This technique is also known as "Just *x* Words," where *x* can be any number you want it to be. Essentially what you are doing is exercising a little self-awareness and coming up with a list of all the words you misuse, misspell, or just get plain wrong. Then we take advantage of your favorite word processor's seek-and-destroy function with a quick Ctrl-F followed by a Ctrl-X (or whatever you happen to use) for every word on your list. As always, "delete" should be your default position here. You really need to justify reinstating any word at all. Obviously you'll need to do a little tidying up afterward, but your message will already be much clearer.

And while we are at it, let's put "ly" into the search function and find all the adverbs. Then—guess what? Delete them too. Adverbs are one of the most overused parts of unedited writing. It's rare that a verb-adverb combination can't be replaced by a single, stronger verb. Don't "speak loudly"—just shout. Don't "walk rapidly"—try striding.

Multiple Passes

The last of the greatest hits is more an overall approach than a specific technique and resembles landing at one of the world's busiest airports, like Heathrow or JFK. Have you ever been delayed by air traffic control and put into a holding pattern? This is basically what we are doing. Start by printing out your work, picking the paper up, and taking it to wherever you would normally sit and read— that cozy armchair by the roaring open fire or the sun lounger on the back deck, perhaps. Read through your work as a reader. Switch off all your critical thinking and just enjoy the reading experience. Now think about what you've just read. Is it doing what it aims to do? If it's a persuasive piece, are you persuaded? If it's nonfiction, do you feel informed and educated? If it's narrative nonfiction, do you believe in the characters and the story? What you've just done is benchmarked it in preparation for the rest of the process. And you've entered the holding pattern.

Now we metaphorically descend five hundred feet. During this time, go back to your desk and pick up your red editing pen, but don't change anything just yet: just circle, underline, or put a question mark or squiggle next to anything you're not sure about. This part of the process is very much reactive, not proactive.

Then we descend another five hundred feet and respond to the squiggles and notes and questions. Change anything you think needs changing, cut unnecessary words, and fix any errors.

Then we go down another five hundred feet and do a line edit—spelling, punctuation, grammar, all the nitty-gritty.

And finally, with air traffic control about to give us the green light to land, we put the pen down, print out the piece again, and head back to the reading chair. This time, the piece should read so much better.

EDITING TIPS

The other collection of gems from my festival days is a list of short but sweet "quotable quotes" on editing. Sitting at the side of the stage, I would make notes whenever something significant was said by three or more authors. So let me present to you the collected thoughts (with a little annotation of my own in parentheses) of some of the world's greatest and most successful writers.

Cut any long sentence into two or three. A fifty-word sentence is better expressed as two twenty-five-word sentences or—even better—two twenty-word sentences with ten words going in the trash where they belong. (I lost count of the number of times I heard variations on this, but it seems no one is keen on long sentences.)

Axe all the adverbs. Put them back if required, but only if required. Do the same to the adjectives. (Again, an almost universal suggestion. I particularly liked the idea from seasoned author, journalist, and editor Sushi Das that your adverbs and your adjectives are your seasoning—the salt and pepper of your writing, if you like. Just as you wouldn't cover your food in salt and pepper, you shouldn't fill up your writing with adverbs and adjectives. Sprinkle them lightly and sparingly, and you will have the desired effect.)

Remove as much punctuation as possible. (Writing is as much a visual form as it is about the actual content, and its appearance on the page has an effect on how the work is read. The logic here is that punctuation breaks up the visual flow and prevents your eyes from moving smoothly along the sentence. If you remove the punctuation, this won't happen. Personally, I quite like punctuation; I think it actually has a purpose. I'll leave that one with you.)

Replace all the negatives with positives. (Looks like someone's been working in an advertising agency here! But in a way, they are right—it is much easier to persuade with a positive statement than it is with a negative one. We all respond better to being asked to do something than being told what *not* to do.)

Replace complicated words with simple ones. (What the kids call a no-brainer, I think.)

Ditch the passive voice altogether. (I think we've already discussed how horrible the passive voice is. When you work in a university, you hear a lot of it, and it never gets any better.)

Reduce prepositions—they break up the flow. (This works on the same basis as the suggested removal of punctuation. The idea is that writing needs to look attractive as well as sound good, and prepositions—all those short, sharp, staccato little words like *in*, *on*, *by*, and *at*—break up the flow. Not so sure myself, and I did wonder if it was more for fiction than nonfiction writing, but enough people mentioned it that I feel I should pass it on. Just the messenger here, OK?)

Use contractions. They make your writing friendlier, more human, so that you sound like you're (not *you are*) a real person. (True.)

Check and recheck those tenses. Make sure they are consistent. Make sure they are correct. She *did* it yesterday, and she *has done* it for decades. And she said she *had done* it for decades. Be especially wary of that last one—reported speech can be a bit tricky. (There are many books and websites that can help you with grammar. It never hurts to check. And if you are unsure, read it out loud—let those ears work their magic.)

Bullet points are part of sentences too. (This is hugely important for writers of nonfiction. There is nothing wrong with a bullet-point list, but you need to remember that, generally speaking, each and every one of the bullet points in your list is an extension of the sentence that introduces them. That means they need to agree grammatically. If the list starts by saying "the things we need to do are," then the rest of the list needs to continue with "reading," "writing," and "sitting up straight.")

Go through your writing by parts of speech—nouns, verbs, adjectives, adverbs. (Another clever trick to give you an analytical edge when editing.)

Assume any mistake is throughout your writing. (Humans are predictable and consistent. If you've misspelled a word on page one, chances are you've misspelled it every time you've used it. So when you find an error, first correct it, but then find all the other places you've made the same mistake and fix them too.)

Be consistent in your changes. (Whether you have moved to more conversational contractions or changed a particular spelling— *colour* to *color*, for example—make sure you have done it consistently. Otherwise, it just looks messy or lazy.)

Get rid of *seems*. It never *seems* to be; it just *is*. (Remember how academics feel the need to hedge? Your nonacademic readers may see this as beating around the bush, prevarication, and a general wishy-washy avoidance of telling it like it is.)

Try really, very hard to get rid of *really* and *very*. You rarely need them. (You might even want to include these words on your hit list for "Just *x* Words.")

Beware of homophones. The principal might be all right, but does he have principles? (If you have words that you consistently have problems with, consider adding them to your "Just *x* Words" list.)

Watch out for *over* versus *more than* and *fewer* versus *less*. (Simple stuff that may merit a place on your watch list if you have problems with it. No shame in that.)

People are *who*, not *that*. (Generally it is "the woman who..." and "the website that...")

If someone "is currently" something, they probably just "are" something. (*Currently* probably belongs on everyone's "to delete" list, along with such other lazy expressions as *at this point in time* or *going forward*. Words and expressions like these are very similar to all the layers of packaging that our food comes in these days. Both of them are unnecessary, both of them belong in the garbage, and ideally both should be avoided in the first place.)

Don't "start to walk." Just walk. (Do the same with any unnecessarily long construction. Don't make your verbs stronger; just strengthen them. Shorter, sharper, and to the point, remember?)

Check your math too. (There's nothing worse than having a beautiful piece of writing with a mathematical error in the middle of it. Check your numbers as well as your words when you edit. And if you're using statistics, make sure they mean something and make sense.)

Read your work out loud. (Couldn't agree more. Trust your ears over your eyes anytime.)

Read your writing in a new format. Change the color, font, size, or device. (Essentially, anything that gives you some sense of detachment from your writing as you shift from the writing phase into the editing phase is good.)

Edit and re-edit at different times of the day. (This is another trick to snap you out of any complacency and force you to look at your work in a new light—literally! In *How to Be a Writer Who Smashes Deadlines, Crushes Editors, and Lives in a Solid Gold Hovercraft*—which is that rare thing, a book that lives up to its title—John Birmingham has some good things to say about when you might write best.)

Never edit justified text. (Even if your publisher or client has specifically asked for justified text, make sure justifying the text is the very last thing you do. Align left, edit, then justify and press Send. When your text is justified, it is impossible to see how many spaces you have put in between words.)

Proofread absolutely everything—words, punctuation, titles, subtitles, table of contents, index, acknowledgments, captions, tables, diagrams, even page numbers! (Good point. If there is an error, no matter how tiny, someone will find it. Do you want to find it, or would you rather your readers found it?)

Avoid distractions when proofreading. (Ideally, avoid distractions when you are doing anything to do with your writing, but realistically, it's OK to have the TV on in the background or people walking past when you are doing the overall edit. Once you get the magnifying glass out and get into the nitty-gritty, though, close the door, turn the music off, and focus. And for God's sake, put your phone down!)

And lastly, remove anything you think the King or Queen might use. (This was only ever said by one writer, but when I heard it, I nearly fell off my chair laughing and thought it worth passing on. If ever you find yourself saying *hereafter, wherein, thereunto, henceforth, aforementioned,* or anything else of a vaguely regal nature, you might want to take yourself outside and have a quiet word with yourself.)

10

SETTING THE SCENE (AND OVERCOMING OBSTACLES)

Creating the perfect environment, both mentally and physically, for engaging and communicating, and dealing with annoying things like writer's block (not that it really exists).

OK, now you know how to write better (and edit too). Where and when you write can also have a huge impact on *what* you write. Some writers are lucky. I remember reading about bestselling Scottish crime writer Ian Rankin being interviewed and enviously referring to fellow Scot and equally pro-lific author Alexander McCall Smith's capacity to write pretty much anywhere—planes, airport lounges, hotels, underwater, and so on. As an aside, Rankin has published more than thirty titles, so he's obviously managing to squeeze the odd bit of writing in here and there too. But the ability to focus and zone out the rest of the world is an acquired talent that takes time.

MAKE SPACE, MAKE TIME

There are some very simple things you can do to help yourself with the task of writing. I don't think it hurts to start a new project with a clean and tidy desk in a light and airy room. Yes, I know this is something we all dream of but never achieve, and I know it will get progressively messier as whatever project you are working on moves forward, but you'd be amazed what returns you can reap on the investment of spending a couple of hours cleaning, tidying, and generally chucking out everything you don't need on your desk and in your office. Your desk really is a bit of a reflection of your mind, so a nice, organized space will make your mind that way too. I always think a tidy desk is akin to pressing the Reset button as you embark on a new writing project. I do the same with my computer desktop when I start something new. And if nothing else, those two hours of tidying and cleaning will count as avoidance and procrastination— the other main skills and interest areas of all good writers.

I also think you need to have somewhere that is entirely your own—Virginia Woolf definitely got it right here. Absolutely no shared desks or spaces and certainly no using a computer that your kids are allowed to play games on.

Serious writing is a bit like joining a gym. As with a good exercise program, you need to get to stage two, by which I mean it's very nice if you do a bit of writing and feel good about what you've written, just as it's good to pop down to the gym, mess around with the machinery for half an hour, and feel good about yourself. This is stage one. But if you are really committed, you will start to feel bad when you haven't written (or done some exercise, for that matter). And that is stage two. You need to be like that.

I've said this before, but you also need to read every day. I like to think that the human brain is a sponge that soaks up words. I am sure the reality is just a tad more complex than that, but as a writer, that's probably all you need to know. Words are the only tools of your trade as a writer, and you can never have enough of them. So how do we get more of them packed in there? How do we find new imagery, metaphors, figures of speech to help us convey our stories? We read.

We should probably just spend a moment or two on the economic environment for your writing. If you still have a "day job," you can smile to yourself and skip this section, but if you're thinking of making the leap to freelancing or are even living under the threat of casualization, I don't have great news for you. Far be it from me to condone and encourage gambling, but if you don't have a second job or a supportive partner, you will probably need to start buying lottery tickets. I remember a very blunt publisher from the north of England with a great sense of humor being asked a question by a trepidatious young writer at a festival once: "Will I be able to make a living out of my writing?" His answer? "At first...no. But then later on...no." Said with a broad smile, of course.

When you write, you also need to develop a thick skin and an optimistic outlook—you need to understand you are in it for the long haul and you must not let the setbacks get to you. Yes, you will get rejected, knocked back, and, in all likelihood, overlooked and even ignored. Often. But you need to remember that it is rarely personal. Someone may have written the same story as you and pitched it ahead of you. A publication may have assigned a staff writer because they saw a big issue that needed a public airing. Maybe something major happened at the publication, and they sent your story—and a whole host of others' stories—into the trash. Just dust yourself off, get back on the metaphorical horse, and keep going.

BE STRATEGIC

It's very important that you think strategically as well as creatively.

Obviously you need to produce well-written, exciting, and imaginative content, but what you do with that content—how you "exploit" it, in the positive sense of the word—and how you make sure it has the best chance of being published is just as important as coming up with the words in the first place. The best time to pitch a story, for example, is when you already have a story online or in print. The same goes for sending in a book proposal. There is no better hook than beginning a pitch for an article with "I don't know if you've seen my piece in today's newspaper, but I am currently working on..." Not only are you demonstrating currency and topicality, but you're giving your potential publisher and business partner a very clear message that you can deliver what you promise.

Being published is very much about relationships. You are much more likely to have a piece accepted by an editor or publisher who knows and trusts you to be able to deliver on time and on word count than you are when you cold-call a publication. Especially as an academic. I hate to be the one to break this to you, but you are working under a degree of difficulty that other writers don't have—namely, the relatively poor reputation that academics have for being able to deliver what they promise. Sure, this is not your fault, and I am confident you will come up with exactly what you have been asked to do, but sadly your predecessors have fallen very short in this department.

AIMING HIGH—WRITING A BOOK

If you want to leap in and write a book, here's an idea: hang out at book launches, book signings, and writers' festivals. These events are great to attend for so many reasons. At a book launch or signing, it won't take you long to work out who is who. The writer will sit at the signing table working hard to sign as many books in as personal a way as they can within the time allotted. Next to the writer will be the publicist who has worked hard to make sure the event is running on schedule. They will be looking a little frazzled but also happy if things are on track. Just behind them will be someone from the bookstore, also looking happy but disheveled from carting boxes of books around. And finally, somewhere slightly out of the action, holding a glass of red and doing very little at all will be the publisher.

No...I kid, I kid! The publisher will be smiling with that zealous smile that you see on the faces of parents at speech night when their kid is onstage collecting a prize. They are the reason everyone else is there.

Writing is a very solitary profession, and sometimes it's nice to know you're not alone, that other people are going through what you are going through and, in fact, have managed to survive and even prosper. At writing events, you'll get inspiration from other writers' success stories, and you may just bump into the person who's going to become your new literary agent or publisher. Never be afraid to approach these professionals—in a way, they expect it at events like this—as long as you get to the point quickly and don't come across as a stalker or serial killer. Even though they hear hundreds of ideas for books, the majority of which will never see the light of day, every publisher worth their salt is constantly on the lookout for the next Simon Schama, Susan Sontag, or Carl Sagan.

PRESCRIPTION FOR WRITER'S BLOCK

I'm not a huge believer in writer's block. What I've found is that, more often than not, writers actually do know why they can't write or, in some cases, don't want to write. The causes are all too commonplace—lack of time to write, boredom with a project that has been dragging on for months, years even, losing track of the endgame, dwindling supplies of motivation, and so on. All of these are eminently fixable, and prevention is much better than a cure. So here's some advice to make sure you're forewarned and forearmed.

Write little but write often. Any writing is good—even half an hour a day. A few words each day is much better than pages and pages of words on Monday followed by a week of silence. Good work will come eventually if you write, but blank pages tend to be very hard to turn into a bestseller.

Keep telling yourself it doesn't matter what you write. All you have to do is produce words that you can fix in the edit. Editing is more important than writing (49:51, remember?), but you can't edit a blank page. So stop staring at one, and just get something down. Don't wait for inspiration to strike.

Make sure you write regularly and in a routine fashion. Ideally this should be in the same place, at the same time, day in, day out. Remember, your writing muscle needs regular exercise if it is to strengthen and develop. Now, of course it is easier for me to say this than it is for you to do it. You'll have competing demands, looming deadlines, and bosses needing reports yesterday, and family life, especially if you have little ones, will encroach on your time too. You just have to do what you can. See it as an investment, albeit a long-term one. The more you put in at the beginning, the greater the rewards will be at the end.

Set yourself some fairly low goals, and celebrate achieving them or even passing them. A couple of hundred words in a session is perfectly acceptable. A few thousand words is a big ask. Going out for a coffee to celebrate achieving your day's word count and even passing it far outweighs sitting at your desk depressed because it is so hard to hit the unattainable mark you've set for yourself. I have a sticky note permanently displayed in the top right-hand corner of my screen. It shows word count to date, word count aimed for, and today's progress. I deliberately set my aim for the day around the thousand-word mark, knowing that I can usually achieve that if I have a day without interruption, and on a good day, I may well pass it. John Birmingham is a big fan of the Pomodoro technique, which divides the day—and the tasks you need to do in it—into nice, easy-to-manage twenty-five-minute chunks (and there's a man who can produce words in volumes that even Costco would be proud of), and I am sure many of you have proudly displayed bright shiny LEGO blocks on your desk during a thesis-writing boot camp. Even though you are well aware that you are playing psychological tricks on yourself, they work time and time again.

Get rid of all physical distractions. One successful writer I know of has an amazing three-story house with huge picture windows overlooking the oldest part of a picturesque European city. Does he sit staring at this picture-postcard view as he writes? Of course not! He wouldn't get anything done if he did. His desk faces the opposite wall, and above it, he has painted a large, black rectangle; this is what fills his field of vision as he writes. Distraction? What distraction?!

Get rid of all digital distractions. You don't need to be checking your email or social media every five minutes. Hollywood producers are not going to come calling, and even if they do, they can wait until break time. And unless you are writing time-sensitive journalism about current events that are taking place here and now, you don't need to know what is going on in the world for a few hours. Turn off every alert, every reminder, everything on your devices that is not immediately relevant to your writing.

Tell people you are writing. Guilt, regular reminders, and even a little good old-fashioned nagging are all great incentives to keep you going. The best and worst question you can ask a writer is "How's the writing going?" It invites excited and passionate discussion of the work in progress while at the same time invoking a fear of the looming deadline and the seemingly snail-like pace of the word counter.

At the end of a writing session, stop halfway through a sentence or paragraph. Don't finish the sentence or paragraph you are working on, but rather leave it hanging there unfinished, and close the laptop with a satisfied sigh. Then, when you next fire up the computer and open the document, you will leap straight into it, finish that sentence in a flash, and be on to the next one before you know it.

Any trick that keeps you in your seat and keeps you writing is good. Music is an extremely common example of this. Lots of writers assemble a large playlist (it may have to get them through six months or more); they press Play on day one, and then, weeks or months later, press Stop when the first draft is finished. More than a few writers seem to favor jazz, although I know of at least one hardcore eighties prog rock fan and another who is heavily into Manchester dance music. However, the consensus does seem to be no lyrics; in a business where you are producing words, other people's words are seen as an outside influence at best and pollution at worst. And at this point, I'd like to say a big thank you to Snarky Puppy, who are probably as responsible for the completion of this book as I am. I really don't think I can start my writing day if I haven't heard "Lingus (We Like It Here)" blasted loud enough for the neighbors to enjoy.

Always have the documents you are working on permanently open in front of you. Let them remind you of their existence and beg for your attention. If they are hidden away in a cupboard or on a

USB stick, they are easy to ignore, but if every time you go to check Facebook or Twitter you are confronted by an unfinished book or article, guilt will kick in.

Writing was never meant to be easy, but it doesn't have to be as hard as some people make it. Get on with it!

3

SPEAKING

11
STANDING AND TALKING

You're going to spend a lot of your academic life doing "chalk and talk," or PowerPoint and chat, or even "Zoom and gloom," as I've heard it called recently. Once you start engaging with the outside world, you're going to be doing even more of it. Presentation and communication skills to help you "talk the talk" are essential.

Public speaking is not rocket science. Some of you reading this book may actually be doing rocket science. You know how hard that is. This is easier. Much, much easier. As much as most people dread it, public speaking is probably the easiest thing you can learn to do. Seriously. All you need to be able to do are four simple things: write, speak, listen, and watch. I told you it was easy! Of course, there are a few extra details, but none of them are that difficult. If you can handle the sort of complex things that make up your day-to-day work as an academic researcher, making a public presentation should be child's play to you.

We've talked about how communication is always a two-way process, a conversation, or a dialogue. Even if you never meet the person you are communicating with, it's still an exchange of ideas.

And you are always talking to, or writing for, someone else. If you give a speech, it's because you want someone else to hear it. It's never just for you. And in this two-way process, the recipient of the communication always matters more than the originator. Once again, I'm going to bring up my favorite ratio. In any act of oral communication, I think the speaker is no more than 49 percent of the process, and the audience is at the very least, but probably more than, 51 percent of the equation.

I've spent more hours than I care to remember standing and talking in front of groups, and I've developed a little trick that I am going to share with you. When I walk out onstage or up to a lectern to address an audience, I always ask myself six questions:

1. Who are you?
2. What do I know about you?
3. What do you know about me?
4. What are you expecting me to tell you?
5. What do I want to tell you?
6. What do I not want to tell you?

What I am doing here is benchmarking my audience. And yes, this does rely on huge assumptions, massive generalizations, and more than a healthy dose of stereotyping, but one, that's all you've got at your disposal, and two, it works. When I first started doing this, I used to go through each question one at a time and carefully consider my answers. Now it all happens in the blink of an eye in a very instinctive way. Remember that communication is always for someone else, right? Well, it is vitally important that your communication be tailored for that particular someone else.

Once you have benchmarked your audience, you can decide

- the **language** you will use: Every group uses different ways of speaking. Some of these differences are quite subtle, and some are quite dramatic. You need to make sure you are speaking in a way that your audience will have no problems understanding instantly.
- how **complex** you can be: The complexity of the ideas you are talking about isn't going to change, but the complexity of the language you use to communicate them is. I often ask PhD students to explain their thesis topics to a hypothetical six-year-old. Once, when the babysitter failed one of my students, this became a real six-year-old—best session I've ever run!
- how **formal or informal** you should be: Who are you addressing—a few colleagues from the department over coffee, the faculty research review committee, a family Christmas gathering, or perhaps the local Rotary Club? Each and every audience requires a different level of formality.
- what **cultural reference points** you can use: I once did some teaching in Hong Kong where the program involved two groups on alternating days. The first group was all the expats, and the second was all the mainlanders and locals. So day one: in went all the *Seinfeld* and *Simpsons* jokes. Day two: out came the *Seinfeld* and *Simpsons* jokes. Day three: well, I think you can guess how it went. The locals hadn't had *The Simpsons* or *Seinfeld* at that stage, so it would have been pointless making those jokes. But for the expats, these areas of common ground provided quite a nice bridge or meeting place. In a similar vein, when speaking internationally, I always keep my eyes on the local news; there's

nothing like a raised eyebrow and a jokey aside about a corrupt local politician to create an instant bond with your audience.

- if there are any **sensitivities** or no-go areas in the situation you are speaking in: Does your research stray into areas that are ethically or politically sensitive? And how "onside" is your audience? Are you addressing an inner-city leftie crowd or the slightly more sedate archbishop's afternoon tea party, for example? I'm not saying you should censor your work; just be aware of the reaction you might evoke in your audience, and if it's going to be controversial, be ready to deal with it.

- if there are any office politics or **power plays** going on in the room: Or, as I like to call it, a good old-fashioned game of spot the dean. There's nothing you can do about this—you can't really ask the dean or head of department to leave—but you do need to be aware of this and factor it in to how you deal with the room. And of course, a dean with a sense of humor is worth two deans with attitude, as the old saying goes.

- who you can **bounce off**: Even in the most difficult crowd, there will be one person who is your friend. Finding them is easy—as soon as you make your first humorous remark or even throw in a joke, they will smile. And you've got them! From then on, they become your conduit to the rest of the room. Hang on to them and don't let them go.

- if there are any **"difficult customers"** in the room: When I started this whole engagement thing, I was sent to address numerous committees. Often, I'd sidle up to a big wooden door with a foreboding sign saying "Meeting in progress" on it. I'd knock and go in, and all but two of the assembled gathering would greet me with a polite smile. The remaining two were invariably older white males in dark suits, always sitting together at the back, arms tightly crossed, hair thinning on top, and sporting an attractive sprinkling of dandruff. You know the types. Their attitude to anything new, certainly anything outward facing like engagement, was always "Don't worry. It's a phase that will pass." You can't ask these people to leave, but you do need to work out how you are going to handle their presence in the room. If you are brave, you can tackle them head-on and try and win them over, or you can ignore them and focus on those who clearly are interested in what you have to say.

You need to run through this process every single time you get up to talk. No two groups are ever the same, even if they look the same on paper. We are human beings, after all—every one of us is different from the next person.

You also need to be prepared for the situation to change and sometimes the possibility that you might be reading it incorrectly. Even the most experienced public speaker can read the room wrong at some point. But what a good speaker does well is think on their feet—a quick route recalibration, if you like. The person you thought was your friend might suddenly take a call and have to leave halfway through. Or you could have misread the dean's hangover from last night's faculty drinks as a look of disapproval when they are totally on your side and love engagement—they just have a whopping headache. When this happens, you have to very quickly repeat the benchmarking exercise you did at the start of the session but take into account the altered circumstances.

I like to think of a good public speaker as being like the performer in a one-person show in the theater. Sure, they stand in front of you all on their own when it's showtime, but a good public performance in any industry doesn't happen without the input of a team of other experts beforehand. In a theater, there might be a director or a dramaturge, set or lighting designers, or voice and movement coaches. The list is endless. As a public speaker, you can use the same approach. If you have an important presentation coming up, why not assemble a support team? All you need are two or three peers or colleagues to listen and respond honestly to your speech—once early on to help you get started, and then once more close to presentation time to fine-tune your speech. Ideally, they shouldn't be close friends, definitely not family, and they probably shouldn't come from your field—when we are familiar with a topic and something is missing, we tend to fill in the gaps without even thinking. What you need is someone a little more detached—a colleague who is not from your area is perfect—who is happy to stop you and say, "I'm sorry. I'm not sure what you mean by that."

GETTING READY

And then we get to preparation. Before you step out onstage or stand at a lectern, you need to be mentally and physically prepared for what is to follow.

Let's start with what would be called preproduction if we were making a film. There are five areas that you need to get sorted in your mind before we even set foot onstage. Three are out of your control, but there are two over which you have total control, so you have no excuse for getting these wrong.

First, the **venue**. My rule is that if the first time you see the venue is when you stand up to speak, you are not trying hard enough. If I am invited to speak somewhere, I will go and visit that venue an hour, a day, even a week beforehand. I'll stand onstage, clap my hands, shout

out loud, listen to the acoustics. I'll go and sit at the back of the audience seating and see what the view from there is. If the venue is inter-
state or overseas, I'll make sure to arrive a day early to check it out. And
if that is not possible, there are always websites with floor plans and
photographs. And if you're booked into somewhere that is absolutely
impossible to see beforehand—say you've hit the big time and you're
due to speak at the Kremlin or the White House—find someone who
has spoken there before and ask them what it was like. There really is no
excuse for entering a venue without knowing what you are up against.

Then you need to think about the **technology** you are going to
be working with. This probably means a projector and screen setup
and maybe a microphone. You get no choice with any of these, but
you do need to be comfortable and familiar with whatever you have
to work with. The projector and screen are easy. Just stay out of
the way of the beam of light. That's all. I am still astonished by the
number of people I see speaking with what looks like a fake tan line
across their forehead or with numbers down one side of their face.
Can't they see the light in their eyes? It must be blinding!

With the microphone, there are a few choices, all of which are
simple to use, but all of which can also be a little uncomfortable and
off-putting if you haven't worn them before. Sometimes you need to
wear a mic when you need amplifying. At other times, the organizers
might be recording or streaming your talk; in this case, you still have
to wear a mic but will be unaware of what it is doing.

Ask beforehand if you are to wear a mic and, if so, what sort. If
you are unsure, ask if you can try it out and if there will be someone
there to help you. If you are worried this makes you look like a nervous first-time speaker, just mention that you'll need a soundcheck.
That will sound professional and impress them!

There are a few different setups you might have to work with:

- **Mic on a stand:** The classic stand-up comedian look. These are nice and easy to use. Just make sure you are twenty-five centimeters or so from the mic, and don't touch it. I can't emphasize this enough: keep your hands off it. There are always qualified grown-ups around whose job is to make sure you sound good. If the mic needs adjusting, ask one of them to do it. Of course, if you do take it off the stand, the advice for the wireless mic (below) applies, but please make sure you don't trip yourself up with the cable.

- **Handheld wireless mic:** Sometimes the microphone will come off the stand—hopefully because it's wireless and you haven't just broken it—and this is also easy to deal with. Same rule of distance from your mouth applies, although the beauty of the handheld mic is that you can actually lower your voice and bring the mic up close to your mouth and use what I call the "sexy radio voice." There is one big disadvantage that you will have with a handheld mic though—the one hand that is holding it might as well be tied behind your back. So if you are with the Department of Aquaculture and your big punchline is "...and the fish that got away was *this* big," you will have to choose between gesturing with one hand only or the last three words being "off mic" and, therefore, unheard. The key, of course, is thinking ahead. You really shouldn't have to deal with a situation like this as, if you're any good, you will have already anticipated only having one hand to work with and worked out an alternative scenario.

- **Small clip-on mics:** The most commonly used mics in university lecture theaters and on television are small mics that need to be affixed somewhere, with a cable threaded through your clothing and a transmitter pack with a belt clip. These are known by a host of different names: the lavalier, pin, bug, lapel, body, or clip mic. Some are quite good, some not so good. Once you're used to them, you can almost forget you are wearing them, but if you've never worn one before, the mic can feel like a buzzing fly in your peripheral vision, the cable can be freezing cold as it passes down the back of your shirt, and if you aren't wearing a belt and the technician is in a hurry, the transmitter pack can be unceremoniously (and uncomfortably) shoved down the back of your underwear. Make sure you dress appropriately. Best not to go commando. And make sure you know how to mute your mic—there's nothing worse than taking a very public bathroom break that is broadcast to the whole of the venue.

- **Over-the-ear, head-worn mic:** The "Madonna mic." Big conference venues are fans of these, as they give really good sound, the mic being positioned right next to your mouth. You'll wear one of these if you are lucky enough to give a TED Talk. Again, to the experienced presenter, these are nothing, but someone never having been miked up this way can feel quite awkward and even self-conscious wearing one for the first time.

Next, find out about your **audience.** You will have to look at and make eye contact with them, and you don't want to waste precious speaking time while your brain attempts to calibrate the room. How big will the crowd be? How you would address twenty people is very different from how you would speak to two hundred people, which is different again from presenting in front of two thousand people.

Where are they sitting? Is the audience set out in a long and narrow shape or spread out wide but not deep into the room? Is the seating terraced or flat? It's also useful to know if there are any VIPs in the house and where they might be sitting, just in case there are any odd group dynamics happening.

Once you have the venue, the technology, and the audience squared away in your mind, you can move on to the two areas that are totally yours to control and with which you can make a significant impact.

Appearances count; how you look sends some vital and potentially strong messages to your audience. So while your next departmental presentation isn't a job interview, in many ways, it isn't so different from one. You wouldn't turn up hoping to impress an interview panel wearing torn jeans and a T-shirt with holes in it, would you? No. So make the same effort when choosing what to wear for a public presentation. It doesn't have to be your Sunday best—unless that's expected—but it has to be appropriate for the occasion. If you want to take this even further, clothing can be used to reinforce a "look"—part of your personal brand. In my case, if you've ever been taught by me, you will know that I have the world's biggest collection of Desigual shirts (and if that isn't a pathetic attempt to get sponsorship, I don't know what is). But make sure you are comfortable too—although I know that balancing this with looking impressive is a big ask. Thesis Whisperer Inger Mewburn from the Australian National University has written extensively and often hilariously on this and with her twin sister even came up with a "clothing taxonomy" for academics that is well worth a read.

How you **sound** is also an area where you can control the message you send. You are a speaker, and your voice is your instrument, your primary tool of the trade. It needs to function at its absolute best (more on this in a second). One of my absolute pet hates is a public speaker or a lecturer starting their presentation with a noisy, guttural clearing of the throat. Often this is followed by "Sorry, just a bit croaky today," and then more coughing and spluttering. I cannot emphasize how unprofessional this is.

WARMING UP

To continue the film metaphor, after preproduction comes the production phase. Once you are totally prepared to present, you move into your "on the day" routine when the first thing you do is warm up physically so that your body and voice are performing at their best. Where, when, and how much you do of this will vary from time to time. If you are giving a TED Talk, for example, you'll probably have a dressing room to warm up in and plenty of time to get ready, but if you're giving an impromptu talk on a Monday morning in the lab, just grab whatever time and space you can.

Start with the **body**. Just as you would never leave the house to go for a jog without warming up, you should never stand in front of people and talk without doing a little bending, stretching, and walking around.

Then focus on the parts of the body that are going to be doing most of the work. Begin with the neck and shoulders—this is where a lot of the action happens when you are expressing yourself in front of an audience. Try some rotations of the neck in both directions and a little light shoulder shrugging.

Moving on to the **face**, cup your hands together and give yourself a dry facial scrub (assuming you're not wearing makeup), even a little gentle slapping. Then try to be like one of those creepy Halloween paintings where the eyes follow you everywhere. Every muscle, right down to those that control your eyes, needs to be warmed up.

Then we get down to the places where the speech comes from, starting with your **tongue**. Try moving it around like a joystick, then blow a few raspberries. Yes—you did read that right. In a serious book about engagement for academics, I did just tell you to blow raspberries.

Next, it's the turn of the **lips**. Try saying "cheese" or doing that old actor trick of going through the consonants followed by the sounds *ee, ah, oo, ay*.

Finally, but probably most importantly, it's time to warm up your **vocal cords**. Try saying a few old-fashioned tongue twisters ("She sells seashells by the seashore," "Peter Piper picked a peck of pickled peppers," that sort of thing) or singing if you like to sing and, of course, rehearsing your speech.

Now, we should look into **voice projection**. If you are not amplified by a mic, or if you are only miked up for recording or streaming but not for amplification, you will need to fill the room by projecting your voice.

First, take a deep breath and...relax. You can't project your voice if you are at all tense. One of the first parts of the body to tense up is the throat, and when your throat tenses up, your voice rises in tone and can sound quite strained and scratchy. Not a great way to exude confidence and authority.

Then warm up in the ways that we talked about before. Anything you can do to get the standing and talking machine that is your body up to optimal operating levels is good.

Next, stand correctly. You'll look like you mean business, and you will get as much air in and out of your body as possible. Your body operates pretty much in the same way as the garden hose you use to water the plants—if it is nice and straight, you will get good water pressure and a nice flow, but if the hose is kinked, the flow will dry up. Similarly, if you stand in anything but a nice straight stance (viewed from both the front and the side), you will be constricting the flow of air in and out and, as a result, restricting how well you will be able to project your voice.

This one is obvious: open your airways and breathe deeply. The amount of air you move is directly proportional to the volume of sound you produce. Big breaths equal big voice. It's as simple as that. Then point your mouth where you want the sound to go—keep your eyes on the prize, as they say. Light and sound are both waveforms and function in very similar ways—if you wanted to illuminate the back of the room, you'd point your flashlight in that direction. So if you want people in the back row to be able to hear, point your sound in their direction. This might sound like stating the obvious, but if you have watched an inaudible presentation by a "carpet talker" or a "ceiling talker," you will know what I mean.

Finally, play tricks on yourself. Use a little self-fulfilling prophecy. Visualize filling the room with your voice in your imagination, and you probably will fill the room with it in real life.

ONSTAGE

Speaking to an audience is a very theatrical thing to do. Essentially, you are the performer of a one-person show, and your slides are your set or backdrop. Being in the same room as your audience, sometimes close enough to be able to reach out and touch them, is incredibly special. It's the magic that makes theater such an immediate art form and so different from film and television. I think a good speaker is aware of this and uses it to their advantage.

I also think good speakers have an **honesty and integrity** about them—nothing should come across as fake or forced. I see public speaking simply as "you plus 10 percent"—10 percent more volume, gestures, and facial expressions, but rarely more than that. It's very important that the underlying "character" the audience is meeting is you—the real you. I am sure you have seen speakers who have a persona they adopt when speaking in public; it's always obvious and never as effective as revealing the real person under the mask. I remember seeing a discussion onstage featuring some political spin doctors where one of the so-called experts suggested, "It's all about honesty. If you can fake that, you've got it made!" The audience howled them down.

Eye contact with your audience is crucial. After all, if you don't know how they are reacting to what you are saying, how can you possibly tailor your talk to suit them? If you're not looking at them, for all you know, they might even be asleep.

I am a big fan of **lightheartedness and humor** when it comes to public speaking. Even the most somber and serious of topics can benefit from a lightness of touch, an injection of humor even. Remember *Macbeth*? What do we get before the discovery of the brutalized body of the King of Scotland? That's right: the drunken porter. Shakespeare knew how to build tension. But while lightheartedness is for everyone, jokes are not. If you can't tell jokes, please don't try.

When I watch someone stand and talk about their work, I like to see someone who is confident, calm, likeable, humble, genuine, credible, authoritative, and in control. You should have no problem being any and all of these things. If you've done your preparation, you will be **confident, calm**, and **in control**. You will have worked out everything that could possibly go wrong and anticipated how you will handle it. If you are just yourself plus 10 percent, you will be **likeable** and **humble**, and you should have no problems being **genuine, credible**, and **authoritative**. You are an expert at a university, so we trust you.

No matter how well prepared your talk is, **you should not have a script** when you speak. Keep in your head rough ideas, bullet points, cue cards, a general idea of the flow and direction, or some sort of mental signposts, but *never* follow a script you have learned by heart. First, if you try to read a script in your head, you'll develop that glazed "autocue in the sky" look where you don't really see the audience in front of you because you are looking at your imaginary script. Second, if you are reading something in your imagination and you lose your place or drop your imaginary pages, it is very hard to get back to where you were. But if you are just moving from A to B to C and you lose your place, all you have to do is a quick mental route recalibration ("Now where was I? Oh yes..."), and you'll pick up from where you left off with no problems.

A good point to note is that public speaking is jazz, not classical. What I mean by this is that no one knows what you are going to say next. As far as your audience is concerned, whatever comes out of your mouth is correct. Just like jazz. If you listen to Mozart or Beethoven, you know what notes are coming next, and if the violinist makes a mistake, you will notice immediately—not because it is necessarily bad, but because it's not how it is *supposed* to be. That doesn't happen in jazz. I can't emphasize this enough: unless you actually say the words "I'm sorry. I made a mistake," no one will ever know you've made a mistake.

Nerves and stage fright are interesting things about which I am often asked. Nerves are actually a good thing. They are a sign that you care about what you are doing. In fact, if you become blasé, that's when you need to worry. It's said that the great knight of the British theater Sir Ralph Richardson used to get so nervous he threw up before every single performance, right up until the end of his illustrious career. I'd rather listen to someone who is clearly passionate about their research but a little nervous when talking about it than someone who thinks they are God's gift to public speaking. Another way of dealing with nerves and stage fright is to tell yourself that it's not actually about you—your message is what counts, and you are nothing more than the messenger. So get over those nerves, and get on with telling people about your amazing discoveries.

And finally, the key to most things is **practice**—whether it's running a marathon or learning the piano or, in this case, public speaking. The more you do, the better you get. It doesn't matter if this is more lab talks or conference presentations or signing up for something like Toastmasters—any practice is good. But forget that whole notion of "practice makes perfect." You're a human being; we are all naturally imperfect. That's what makes us so interesting. Don't waste your time trying to practice until you get it right. That's impossible. Just practice until you can't get it wrong.

In writing and editing, we talked about making sure every word on the page is there for a reason. There's a great quote attributed to the Argentine writer Jorge Luis Borges that translates to standing and talking: "Don't talk unless you can improve the silence." Let's make sure we always improve the silence.

12
PRESENTING ONSCREEN

Sometimes it's impossible to be in the same room
as your audience. So whether it's a pandemic
or just a conference budget that doesn't run to
an airfare that's preventing you from meeting
face-to-face, the art of presenting onscreen
is now something we all need to master.

We really do live in interesting times; during the course of writing and editing this book, presenting onscreen—by Zoom or Skype or other means—went from being a bit of a last resort to becoming the absolute norm for engaging with others. And all within a matter of a few weeks. In the past, you wouldn't have hesitated to jump on a plane and go to a conference or meet for a coffee and a chat, but now our first instinct is to turn on the webcam, log in, and start talking. And there seems to be little likelihood of this changing, certainly in the near future. So if presenting onscreen is now one of the key tools of our trade as communicators, let's make sure we do it well.

The technology might seem a bit daunting at first, but it is actually relatively simple to master. Let's start with the **camera**; every laptop and a lot of PCs come with a webcam built in. Some are

OK—but often only OK—whereas some leave a lot to be desired. Plugging in an external webcam is something worth trying as it gives you a lot more flexibility in how you are seen onscreen. With these things, you really do get what you pay for, so try to stretch your (hopefully tax-deductible) budget to its limit. You should be looking for as high a resolution as possible and something that is physically flexible—a long cable, ideally with a built-in stand, plus the ability to be mounted on a tripod. The more it can do, the more you can do with it. Set it up at eye level, and try and position it as close as you can to the active speaker window onscreen—this will make it look as though you are making eye contact with your audience.

Then you should think about **sound**. Your computer will probably have built-in speakers and a microphone, but—as with the camera—their quality isn't necessarily the best. Again, external may be the best way to go. Try using the earbuds/microphone setup you use with your phone or maybe invest in a call center–style headset so that the microphone can be close to your mouth. I have a standing desk, and I like to use a Bluetooth headset so I am not physically tied to the one spot and can move around. Experiment a little and find the one that feels and sounds best for you.

Lighting comes next. If you just turn on the lights in your room and sit in front of your webcam, chances are you're going to look a little flat and washed out. With a little effort, it's not that hard to look more professional onscreen. Ideally you need three separate light sources, each of which plays a very specific role. First you need what's called a key light. Essentially, it's a fairly direct light source that throws a few shadows across your face—making your nose stand out, for example—to show that your face is three-dimensional. You position it off to one side of your face and slightly in front of you.

Then, because the key light can be quite harsh, you use a second softer light from the other side of your face—called a fill light—that fills in those shadows a little but doesn't remove them entirely, so your face looks like it has depth but isn't covered in harsh shadows. If you don't have a second light source, an old trick is to reflect the key light so that it also functions as the fill light using a piece of white board positioned where you would place the fill light. Lastly, you need to give the picture some depth and separate yourself from the background. The traditional television studio approach to this is to have a light from behind that strikes the back of your head, called a backlight, but you can get a bit creative with this. If you have a reading lamp, for example, place it at the back to one side of the shot so its light falls across the wall or bookshelf or whatever is behind you. Really, anything that lights the background separately is good. I use a setup of seven lights whenever I have to present on camera: a key, a fill, a highlight just to lift the face a little, and four backlights to pick out various parts of my office to make it look interesting and to separate me from the background. But just experiment—find something that looks good for you. And if your technology is limited— say you're stuck with just one big light, for example—remember that reflected light is always best. Try bouncing your light off the ceiling to give you a soft, indirect light, which is much easier on the eye than a single harsh spotlight.

And while we are stealing from the world of film and television, it wouldn't hurt to think about **location**. Your laptop can move, so why not take it somewhere interesting? Find yourself a good-looking background—nothing too busy but not too bland either. Maybe even something that has some resonance with your field of research; laboratories make for great backgrounds if you're a scientist, for example.

As a general rule, always try to avoid flat and featureless; they make for very boring backgrounds. And there is no reason why your laptop has to face the wall at a ninety-degree angle. Aim for something a little less obvious and predictable—maybe a rakish sixty-degree angle? Just make sure there is nothing controversial or personal that can be seen onscreen. Recently, I was part of a team producing COVID-19 training for the medical profession, and we quickly got into the routine of getting clinicians to check for patients' personal details on the noticeboards behind them before we started filming.

A lot of the software available for video conferencing allows you to use a virtual background or even do the full green-screen effect where you electronically remove everything of a specific color and drop in an alternative background. I've seen it used a fair bit, but in most cases, it just looks tacky. And in all likelihood, you'll have that "halo" effect—you move your head quickly and a bizarre shadow, like a very bad aura, seems to follow you a split second later.

It's a mistake easily made, but if you're sitting in front of a predominantly blue background, try not to wear blue clothes. You risk fading into the background, and if you decide to go with the virtual background effect, you may *literally* disappear into the background as the technology fails to distinguish between the blue of your shirt and the blue of the wall behind you. Aim for a contrast between you and your background.

It also wouldn't hurt to give a moment's consideration to the **size of shot** you are using. There are a range of shots that a camera can capture. When you are Zooming or Skyping, you are probably going to be seen in a mid-shot (head and shoulders) or a close-up (face only). This means any big, larger-than-life gestures that normally work in the classroom or lecture theater are going to be lost onscreen.

For onscreen presentations, I tend to stand back from the camera a bit in a mid-shot that verges on a wide shot, but I am always aware that I am having an intimate chat with the audience—not giving a full-blown theatrical performance.

If you want to show **documents** when you are presenting onscreen, make sure you have everything you need all cued up and ready to go. You should be able to just casually click the "share screen" button and have the file appear onscreen effortlessly. It's not a great look if you are fumbling around while everyone sits and waits.

When you present to a camera, you will not be able to gauge the **audience reaction** that you would in a room full of people. Your monitor is going to be full of tiny little screens showing people whose microphones are muted, which means you can't really see people's faces and you can't hear their voices. Again, this is not something you can change but is rather something that you just get used to. Oddly, in real life, the bigger the audience, the bigger the reaction, but onscreen this is reversed: the larger the crowd, the smaller their images become and the less you can see of their reactions. And of course, all this relates to speaking on camera live. There are odd occasions when you have to record yourself and send it in; then the only reaction you get is the blinking red light above the camera. Have a think about the setup you'll be using, and get creative; see if there's a way you can involve the audience. Is there a chat box, for example, or does the software allow for polling?

As with most things, the key to presenting well onscreen is to practice. All software offers you the option to preview what you are going to share with the world, so take that opportunity to make sure you look your best. And rehearse on camera if you have a formal presentation to give. If you really want to test things thoroughly, you can always Zoom or Skype yourself; if you have more than one device—a phone or a tablet as well as your computer, for example—try setting up a second account and having a meeting with yourself to see what you look and sound like.

And lastly, far be it from me to add to your to-do list, but you will probably have to reorganize your life a little around your on-camera time. This might mean a closed, possibly even locked door, signs saying that you are "on air," or even a diversionary bone for the dog to quietly gnaw on. The first Fortune 500 CEO to be interrupted by a toddler was cute, but since then, the novelty has definitely worn off.

4

PROFILING

13
PLATFORM 9¾

We've established that you're an expert who knows a lot. So how do you turn that knowledge base into that magical thing that everyone is after, a platform?

Apologies for the shameless Harry Potter reference, but it got you looking, didn't it?! Sorry, but this is quite an important chapter, and I didn't want you getting lazy and skipping it.

The mantra of academia used to be "publish or perish." Being seen, read, and cited in academic journals, especially quality academic journals, was the be-all and end-all of a researcher's life. While that still applies for the academic side of your life, there is now a new and possibly more pressing imperative for you to live by: "Be visible or vanish." These days, it's all about having a public profile, hopefully a very high public profile, sometimes called your platform.

A platform is a fairly loosely defined way of encapsulating everything that makes you an authority, an expert, or a go-to person in the eye of the public. Propose a book to a trade publisher, for example, and one of the first questions they may ask is, "What is your platform?"

Over the years, I've developed what I call a tasting menu—a fairly diverse list—of things that collectively can contribute to your platform. We'll look at most of them in greater detail later, but for now, just cast your eye over this menu and make a mental note of what you'd like to try out as a new academic.

BUILDING YOUR PLATFORM

The first three stages on the list are compulsory. You have to start online, and you have to develop some sort of online presence. Apart from those three, you don't have to do each stage in the order I suggest, though it works best that way. And you don't have to do every one, but it helps if you do.

1. **Start a blog, Twitter, Instagram, TikTok, website, etc.** Establish a toehold in the online world.
2. **Build up friends, followers, etc.** Take your digital presence to the next level.
3. **Take part in forums, join communities, etc.** Be more active online; become a bit of a "player."
4. **Get out there and give talks.** When I say "give talks," I don't want you talking to the lab, the department, or the faculty. That's too easy. Get out there and talk to neighborhood groups, schools, festivals, book clubs, historical associations, even Lions, Rotary, or Apex clubs. Talk to people who don't know you and have no idea about your work or area of expertise. If you can take a group of disinterested strangers and, after thirty to forty minutes of intelligent chat, have them smiling and nodding and asking interested questions, you are a good communicator. Just make sure you do everything we discussed in the speaking chapters, and you'll be highly sought after on the speakers' circuit before you know it.

5. **Get onstage at festivals, conferences, public events, etc.**
   When we're not locked down by a virus, pretty much every
   town and city on this planet has a full schedule of science weeks,
   writers' festivals, ideas-based events, public conversations, and
   the like, and they are always looking for guest speakers, hosts,
   interviewers, and facilitators. And even the online equivalents
   can offer some limited networking opportunities. So prepare
   your pitch, and make contact with the organizers. You probably
   won't start by giving the keynote to thousands of people in the
   local town hall, but you could quite easily introduce the person
   who does.

6. **Go to book launches, gallery openings, festival launches.**
   Essentially, hang out where you will rub shoulders with people
   who matter. Or, for a while longer at least, rub "virtual" shoulders with them. But make sure you talk to them. Make yourself
   known. It's everyone's pet peeve, I know, but you need to do
   some good old-fashioned networking.

7. **Write letters to the editor.** In a sense, this is quite an old-
   fashioned thing to do, and this step can often be skipped by
   going straight to pitching an opinion piece, but they are still
   quite a satisfying writing exercise. If something comes up in the
   world you are an expert in, or even if something deeply personal
   gets you fired up—if they are going to bulldoze your kids' favorite park, if they are going to take half your backyard for a runway
   extension, if your favorite shopping center is going to be graced
   with a betting shop, a casino, or a brothel—then get angry and
   put pen to paper. Quite short, quite traditional, and quite formulaic (always a beginning, a middle, and an end—no fancy
   postmodernist forms here—and strong declarative sentences), a

letter to the editor can be a call to action, a challenge, or a public questioning of the status quo and can often be the start of something big. Of course, this does bring up that vexed question of the border between your professional life and your private life. It's also important to check your university's policies and guidelines on public comment, especially when you are commenting on something outside your field of expertise.

The next two items refer to countries where there is a healthy public radio culture. If you are lucky enough to live in one of these places, enjoy it and take advantage of it. If you're not (and I've taught in enough of these places to know how dire "ordinary" radio can be), I feel for you. With any luck, the digital, streaming, podcast-driven audio revolution will come to your rescue at some point soon.

8. **Call in to a radio show.** Have the radio on in the office, the car, or at home, and when something comes up in the discussion that you know about, care about, or just have a strong opinion about, don't hesitate to pick up the phone and call in. If you get through, you'll probably talk to a producer, who will quickly assess what you've got to say and whether you are sane. You'll be put on hold and listen to the live radio for a while until suddenly you're on air. That's right—the world is listening to you and what you have to say. Talk in short, easily editable grabs; don't talk over the host, even though they may well rudely interrupt you; and be light, breezy, and interesting, no matter how deep and dark the topic is. Do this a few times, and before you know it, you will probably...

9. **Be invited to appear on radio.** At this point, you are now in the enviable position of being a go-to person. You've called in a few

times, you've shown that you are an expert in a particular field, and your name and contact details have been noted down in the digital equivalent of the producers' little black book. Next time "your" issue comes up again in the news and they need expert commentary, guess who they'll be calling? It might be ridiculously short notice, it might be at really inconvenient times of the day, and it might mean you changing your policy of not answering calls from unknown numbers, but it's all in a day's work for an expert gun for hire. And with podcasting on the rise, it probably wouldn't hurt to make yourself known in this world too.

10. **Pitch opinion pieces.** Once you have made a name for yourself as an expert and have a strong digital presence, you can pitch an idea for an opinion piece on a topic that is close to your heart. If you are visible enough, you may even be invited to write an opinion piece. With four hundred to eight hundred well-written words, you can get into the opinion pages or their online counterparts and get people thinking, talking, and—we hope—acting. The University of Sydney's Tim Soutphommasane, for example, wrote some very interesting commentary about the racism that the COVID-19 outbreak brought to the surface in Australia. And on a very welcome note, there's even a tiny possibility that this could be the first time that you will be paid to write—a very exciting milestone in the life (and bank account) of a new academic. (For more on pitching and writing these, see "Newspapers and Magazines," page 155.)

11. **Write short articles.** A few opinion pieces and a high public profile will then see you pitching and writing short articles (around one thousand to fifteen hundred words) for newspapers and

magazines, things like "explainers"—an article supplying expert background commentary on an issue that is in the public eye. The complexities and general oddness of the electoral process in the United States always produce some very good examples of this. (See "Newspapers and Magazines" for more.)

12. **Write book reviews.** You can write book reviews at any point in your career, so this is more of a floating menu item. Book reviews are a great level playing field: one Saturday morning, I opened the paper to the books pages and saw two book reviews side by side—same word count, same prominence and placement—one written by the vice-chancellor of the university I was teaching at, the other by a PhD student I was working with. Book reviews are also important because they are typically read by three groups of people—people looking to buy a book and doing their market research, people who just enjoy the book review form, and, by far the most important of the three, publishers. Publishers need to know what is being said about their books, so they will read the review pages with something akin to religious devotion. And they have very long memories, so if you have any long-term aspirations to having a book published by a commercial publisher, write a few good book reviews (well-written reviews, not necessarily complimentary ones), and when you come to pitch your own book— even years later—you may be remembered. So find out what titles are coming out in your field in, say, two to three months, and email the books or arts editor of your local paper. Very briefly tell them who you are and why you're interested in reviewing the titles in question, and show them a sample of your writing.

13. **Write longer articles.** These are pieces of two thousand to three thousand words that appear in newspaper weekend

supplements or in the pages of quality magazines. These could be feature stories offering an informed reflection on big issues but not necessarily newsy issues. Here you will have the luxury of time and distance to look back at an event or a movement and give a more nuanced, contemplative view. (More on these in "Newspapers and Magazines.")

14. **Then, of course, comes your first book.** The dream of most writers and academics. As well as traditional publishing, ebooks, print-on-demand technology, and new versions of self-publishing offer some very exciting alternative opportunities for long-form writing.

15. **Be open to all other opportunities** such as exhibitions, documentaries, TV series, feature films, theme park rides, arena spectaculars, and so on. If you are interested in hearing the little-known story of how Australian women became the first in the world to gain full political rights, for example, you should watch *Utopia Girls: How Women Won the Vote*, a documentary presented by La Trobe University historian Clare Wright. And if you want to find out about the groundbreaking work of Singapore's Future Cities Laboratory, just tune in to their podcast series. We really have no idea what is coming next, other than knowing it will almost certainly be technology driven, in terms of sharing our research, so the operative words there are "be open to." And I didn't make up those last two opportunities, by the way—serious researchers had a lot of fun developing the theme park ride Mission: SPACE at Florida's Walt Disney World Resort and the arena spectacular *Walking with Dinosaurs*.

CONTROLLING THE PIGEONHOLE

We are all going to be pigeonholed in life, so why let others decide how you're going to be remembered? Why not take control of your own pigeonhole and come up with your own personal brand?

Try this quick exercise that I often call "controlling the pigeonhole." Imagine the local radio station has called you up to ask for your opinion, fact checking, background, or commentary on the news of the day, and you're on hold waiting to go on. Think about what sorts of issues could come up that would make this a reality. Where could you fit into the news of the day?

Now imagine what the host is going to say into the microphone by way of introduction: "And on the line we have..." You're allowed ten words tops, so every word has to count. What ten words will describe your expertise and its relationship to the story while being instantly understandable by your average radio listener?

This is a very useful exercise and one that in the long term can help you achieve a more focused, strategic public profile, name a blog or a website, or even just stay in the public's mind long after your fifteen minutes of fame are up.

Once you have chosen your own ten words, go to the web page of your local talk radio station, and look back at some of the interviews with experts they have archived there. The transcription will always begin with a short, punchy introduction of the interviewee. How does yours compare?

• • •

So that's it—these things that separate you from all the other forgettable "old" academics and help you stand out as a new academic. As

I said before, these are only serving suggestions. You can make your own list, you can reorder this one, you can add and subtract as you see fit, but the more you do, the better your chances are of being noticed, being listened to, and achieving one of the holy grails of contemporary academia—impact.

14

ASK AN EXPERT

You're an expert. You know interesting stuff. We are interested in interesting stuff. Don't make it more complicated than it needs to be.

Anyone can have a platform, but there are two ways to get people to really pay attention to you. One is to make a lot of noise (which I hope none of us will stoop to), and the other is to know more than the rest of us—to be an "expert."

In academia, you are used to being part of a long food chain of expertise and authority. It's hierarchical and old-fashioned. You have to constantly defer to those ahead of you while taking every opportunity to show that you are smarter and know more than those behind you. But take one step outside the academy, and the world's view of you is different. You have a PhD! You are a trusted expert whose authority is certainly listened to and, in most cases, believed. You are also allowed to have an opinion—not only on your topic but on other topics outside your particular field of interest. In fact, you are not so much allowed as expected to have such an opinion. People want you to be a pundit.

I remember a student years ago who had done some research into something like politics and philosophy in Paris between 1914 and 1968 (I forget the details). She'd written a piece for the non-academic media, and a radio station had picked up on it. On the way to the radio station, she read that, overnight, the then president of France, Nicolas Sarkozy, had sacked a few more female members of his government—something he was renowned for at the time. Guess what happened? The radio host looked at the cheat sheet for the interview, saw the words *Paris* and *politics*, and dived straight in: What did the student, as a woman specializing in this field, a Francophone, and an expert in French politics, think of what Sarkozy had done? Was she shocked? Had she seen it coming?

The student had two choices. The first would have been the classic academic response—"I am sorry. This is outside my area. You'd be better off asking Professor Such-and-Such, who is the acknowledged expert in the field." This would have resulted in radio silence, general embarrassment, and a mental note never to invite her back again. But her second choice—and the one that she made—was to acknowledge that not only was she an expert in *le monde français* but that she also read the French press closely every day and—*Mon dieu!*—she did indeed have a very strong opinion on this very questionable practice. Guess who became a bit of a go-to person on all things French and political for a while?

Imagine you are researching something like the cellular processes responsible for retinal ganglion cell injury and recovery in the human eye (and if I've lost you there, just seek out Eamonn Fahy's winning Three Minute Thesis competition entry online). Even though your research is incredibly focused and detailed, you are still allowed to talk about the bigger picture and the possible applications. You don't have to become the generic scientist in the lab coat talking about all science, but if your research offers us a ray of hope of eventually conquering a particularly horrible disease at some point, let's talk about that. And if all your results aren't in yet, if you haven't dotted every *i* and crossed every *t*, don't worry. We don't mind a few dreams and aspirations: "While it's a long way in the future, I'd like to think that we might be moving closer to a cure for..." Dr. Darren Saunders, a cancer biologist from the University of New South Wales, is very good at doing this. If you have a moment, search out a great discussion he was part of on Australian Broadcasting Corporation Radio National's *Big Ideas* on how to combat pseudoscience with better science communication.

Really, outside the academy, the rule is this: whoever in the room knows the most about a subject is the expert. We don't have the time or the patience or even the inclination to contact Professor Emeritus So-and-So of the Berlin Institute for whatever. We're talking about something related to your topic, you know enough for the conversation, you are here and available right now, so you'll do. You're the expert. Not what you're used to, I know, but don't worry: rarely is anyone out to get you or to set you up with difficult questions to show that they know more than you. So go on: tell us what you think.

In a way, you need to think of yourself as a brand. Now, while you are not Coke or McDonald's, in some ways, you are like them—you offer a coherent and presentable picture to the world in the same way that they do. And you trade off that brand. They do it by selling soft drinks or burgers, and you do it by discovering amazing things and telling the world about them. So think of it this way: you represent your own personal brand, and part of your job is to do PR for that brand. Which is where being an expert comes in. In fact, it wouldn't hurt to take a few moments to work out what your brand is. How do you want to be known? What topics do you feel qualified or confident to talk about in public? And despite the idea that you really can talk about anything, are there any areas you'd prefer to leave to colleagues? Remember how being pigeonholed is not such a bad thing, as long as you maintain control?

I know this chapter has turned into more of a pep talk than a guide, but that's because you already know more than enough on your topic for the purposes of talking to the rest of us. You just need to shake off any academic hang-ups you might have, open your mouth, and start speaking. And hurry up! Not only are we dying to hear from you, but if you don't share your ideas, expertise, and opinions with us, there are plenty of others who will.

15
YOUR GOOGLEABILITY

The "Do Not Pass Go, Do Not Collect $200" moment.
It's time to move on from "publish or perish" and
instead turn toward "be visible or vanish."

This is where it all begins. Online. Nowhere else, just online. When journalist and editor Sushi Das ran the opinion pages for one of Australia's highest profile daily newspapers, she used to do guest lectures for me. She would regularly stand in front of groups of PhDs or early career researchers and say to them, "You are exactly the exciting, new voices I am looking for. I am sick of the usual suspects, the same old people who are dragged out to offer so-called expert commentary time and time again. I have had enough of them. I want you!" She would pause for effect as they all sat up straight in their seats and bathed in the collective flattery they had just received. Then she would continue. "But how am I going to find you? I want to quote you, interview you, commission you, but to do so, I need to be able to find you. How do I do this? I'll give you a clue. The answer starts with *G* and ends with *oogle*."

Opinion-page editors do it. Radio-show producers do it. Even television producers looking for an expert to sit on the couch on breakfast TV do it. They all google.

THE GOOGLE TEST

During my teaching, I will often do "the Google test" with my students. It's a very simple process but tells you a lot about your googleability (OK, this is probably not a real word, but let's just work with it.). So, let's try it now. Open a browser on your device or computer. Then go to Google or any other search engine. Now I want you to go looking for yourself in three different ways.

First, put your name into the search engine. What you are hoping to see is, of course, lots of references to yourself, all ideally at the top of that very first page of search results. If you share your name with a movie star or sporting hero, this one's not going to be easy, but even if you do, there are ways around that.

Then, while you are looking at the page of results with your name on it, click on "Images" and see if your happy, smiling face comes up. Again, we are looking for a page full of pictures of you.

These first two Google tests are useful, but mostly as a warm-up to the main attraction. Sure, people will often google people whose names they already know, but the acid test is if you can be found because of what you know rather than who you are.

So third—and most importantly—put six words into the search engine. Six words and no more. Six words that encapsulate you, your life, your interests, your expertise, and your personality. That's right— you are controlling your pigeonhole again! You're not allowed to use your name; that would be cheating. What you're doing is replicating what all those radio, newspaper, and TV editors do every time they need an expert to quote, interview, or even commission to write or speak on a particular topic. The easiest way to do this is to see it from their point of view—what might happen in the news or the public conversation that demands *your* expertise? You truly have a public profile if Google offers a page full of references to *you* as a result of these six keywords. I imagined I was commissioning something for an anniversary of the French Revolution and needed someone local I could ask. I put "French revolution history Australian expert" into Google and came up with Peter McPhee. And I suspect I didn't even need the word *history*. If you have any intention of engaging with audiences outside academia, having a digital presence—an online brand—is pretty much compulsory.

USE SOCIAL MEDIA

I could give you a list of all the places you can engage online these days, but it would be out of date before the ink was dry. The digital landscape is one of the most fluid and rapidly changing environments on the planet. The easiest way of approaching it is to have a look at all the different ways you might use the online channels that make up social media and decide what you want to achieve. Here are just some of their uses for a new academic.

Staying in touch. Social media is now probably the best way to keep up-to-date with what's happening in the world. Topical stories are broken, debated, and disseminated online in forums like Twitter. So when you get around to writing stories for the media about your work, showing where it fits in the big scheme of things is very important to making your story relevant.

Increasing your visibility. Public awareness of your work is so important—you need the generous and supportive general public to know about you. Visibility also has repercussions in your academic life. You might spend weeks working on that massive grant application, but what do you think will be the first thing your assessors do? That's right—even they will look for you online before delving into the hundreds of carefully written pages you've sent them, and they may even filter out candidates with no online presence straightaway.

Gaining new audiences. Social media is an incredibly easy place to find new audiences for your work. If you can embrace this rapidly changing world, the gains you can make in audience reach are almost limitless. Just look at what astrophysicist Kirsten Banks has achieved on TikTok, for example.

Making a name for yourself. Whether we like it or not, the world is a very selective—if not competitive—place, and familiarity is often the key to success. Becoming a bit of a household name in your field will open doors and gain you access to people and places that would otherwise be impossible.

Finding research subjects. Sometimes you will need participants for your research, and social media is a great way to find them. There was a time when a researcher looking to the public to participate in their research would place ads in newspapers only to receive a handful of replies. Today, the word can be spread so quickly and widely through all your social media channels that you will easily fill your quota before you know it.

Being contacted. The digital world is also perfect for establishing a point of contact. These days, no one in their right mind would make their phone number or address public, and it's very easy to get lost in the crowd on your university website, whereas a social media presence with direct messaging or an email address or even a pop-up or drop-down box where people send you their details is both fully accessible yet entirely safe, secure, and even anonymous.

Communicating your results. While you still have to write the journal articles and conference papers for your academic peers and colleagues, social media is a highly effective way to communicate the results of your research to the rest of us. Of course, this is not in the same degree of detail and depth, but that's easily dealt with— you just offer links to your full research papers for those who are interested. So summarize your amazing discoveries in a blog post, tag a few fellow experts with public profiles, and email others with a link to the piece, and before you know it, your audience will start to grow.

Building community. Social media is perfect for staying in touch with and getting support from your peers and colleagues. Virtually every social media channel includes some sort of provision for discussion groups or forums, some public, some closed. Who hasn't attended a conference lately where the first things you see on the screen at the opening address are the various hashtags and ways of following the conference proceedings and staying in touch? And the best way to survive life during a PhD? Just follow #PhDChat or #PhDLife.

Looking to the future. Social media is the perfect place to sow the seeds for future publication. If you have long-term aspirations to write a book for commercial publication, a strong social media presence—and thousands of friends and followers—forms a solid foundation for a proposal to a publisher.

Promoting yourself. This is not a bad thing, people! There is nothing wrong with self-promotion, especially for career development, as long as you do it right. If you've discovered something amazing, get online and tell us. But please don't do fake modesty—all that "I am deeply humbled" crap. No one buys it!

Avoiding the vacuum. We've already dealt with the great moral, ethical, and financial imperatives—you can't own knowledge, and you are genuinely discovering things on someone else's dime—as well as the more pressing imperative for you to take part in the public conversation. You owe it to the rest of us to share what you know. If you don't, you are condemning us to be forever misled, misinformed, and manipulated. And again, where better to address this than via social media?

• • •

I add to this list from time to time and when teaching often go around the class asking if anyone has ideas they'd like to add. I had a few recently that are worth adding. First was someone who simply said, "I just want to stand out from the crowd." Absolutely nothing wrong with that. Then I had someone who was looking for a job— again, a perfectly good thing to do. And then the most recent (and probably the funniest) was "I just want to have a bit of a rant."

Yes, the digital world is, most decidedly, the perfect place to have a good, old-fashioned rant. I've mentioned one of the current buzz-words going around academia—*impact*. This is the idea that not only should you be measuring the results of your research in their own right but that you also need to look at the flow-on effects of those results in the wider world, be that in academia or out in business, industry, or the community. To quote Lina Duque, a social media strategist, in the *Harvard Business Review*, "It doesn't matter whether you have a small following at first. Becoming a smart user of social media can help you translate your research into impact."

5
COMMUNICATING

16
WRITING ONLINE

Writing online—from a handful of characters to a whole heap of words—is a specialized world with its own rules, customs, and more than a few quirks.

The online world is full of huge and exciting opportunities. As early as 2013, linguist David Crystal saw that "The Internet has given us ten or fifteen new styles of communication... I see it all as part of an expanding array of linguistic possibilities." And so should you.

WHERE TO SHARE

There are so many different ways you can share your ideas online, and soon we're going to look at just three of these possibilities—tweeting, blogging, and websites. Broadly speaking, they represent differing approaches to writing in the digital world: short and sharp, dynamic and casual, formal and static.

Of course, in many cases, you don't even need words. If your research lends itself to visual imagery (and you'd be surprised what research can fit into this category if you try a little lateral thinking), an image-based channel such as Instagram might be right for you. I've seen some amazing examples of research projects brought to life without a word in sight.

And if your work is not just pictures but moving pictures, then YouTube or Vimeo might well be for you. Again, you'd be surprised what makes for interesting online video content. And it doesn't have to be a two-hour epic—sometimes shorter is actually better. Even an imaginative slide presentation with a voiceover can make for perfectly viewable content. And if your budget has allowed you to produce something more exciting—an animation, for example—why not share that with the world?

There's a great new competition in Australia that is really starting to take off called Visualise Your Thesis. Researchers have to produce a sixty-second PowerPoint presentation that encapsulates some aspect of their research. I've seen some very impressive entries that have embedded sound, video, and animation to create something eye-catching and engaging. These make great content for a YouTube channel. Seek out the University of Melbourne's Rachel Pollitt and her presentation "Mathematics and Assessment in Early Childhood Education" on Vimeo—a serious topic brought to life with little more than an iPhone, a glass coffee table, and a few bits of paper. I think you'll be impressed.

Then there are the big production numbers—podcasts and vodcasts—where you can really bring your work to life. More work, more resources, and sometimes a bit of cash are required here, but not as much as you might think.

HOW TO WRITE ONLINE

So how do you write online? The answer is simple—take everything

I told you about writing better and dial it up another 20 percent. So short becomes shorter—much shorter. Get to the point in your very first sentence. "Eye-catching and interesting" becomes "dramatic and amazing." And so on. You are dealing with an audience with a low level of commitment whose members are used to browsing rather than following linear pathways. And this is without factoring in the constant threat of the clicking finger—the finger that can take your reader to eBay or Amazon or anywhere else they care to roam with no more energy than tapping a screen or a mouse button requires. In terms of grabbing and keeping the attention of your readers, this environment is as competitive as it gets.

In academia, you are taught to write up your results thus: "I came up with a hypothesis, then I did this experiment, and then I did another experiment, then I tested my ideas some more, and so on until [dramatic fanfare] *ta-da*! I proved this." If you wrote this way online, very few of your readers would make it to your dramatic conclusion, no matter how exciting or groundbreaking it was. Online, we don't have the patience to wait for your big reveal at the end. Instead, you need to tell us up front: "I proved this! And here's how I know it..." Your readership may still dwindle and trail off over the course of your writing, but at least the vast majority know what it is you've achieved from the very beginning. A few more of them may stay along for the ride if the opening line—the "hook," in journalistic terms—is particularly interesting.

THE RULES OF ENGAGEMENT

When you speak out in public—no matter where or how you do it—take a look at your university's rules, regulations, and policies on how they'd like this to happen. Every university is different, and they can range from the highly enlightened and supportive all the way to the downright old-fashioned and draconian. But the bottom line is, while you are not claiming to formally represent your institution in public, the fact that you are an expert employed by them does imply some representation, certainly in the public's eye.

So ask what the rules are. Some places won't mind at all and will even be delighted if you take a very controversial position in the public conversation, whereas others will require you to go through a maze of bureaucracy and paperwork that will make commenting on current affairs nigh on impossible. I once taught at one of the oldest and most esteemed universities in the United Kingdom where I foolishly assumed contribution to the public debate would be encouraged as some sort of civic duty. When the students there explained to me the six-month-long process of approvals and supervisory committees that even a simple letter to the editor would have to undergo, even my cynicism toward academic bureaucracy was stretched to its limits.

And always remember that any form of online distribution of your words and ideas is publishing in the legal sense and so subject to a number of laws including, very importantly, the laws of defamation and of copyright.

• • •

Now, let's look at three different ways of communicating your research to the outside world where your audience is using a phone, tablet, or other digital device.

17

TWEETING

Life, the universe, and everything...in 280 characters.

The most successful and best-known example of short-form writing right now has to be Twitter. Tweeting, whether it be the original, hardcore 140 characters or the more recent 280-character version, can be a great way to communicate ideas. It can be daunting at first—especially when you realize that it is not words, not even letters, but characters that are being counted so that every comma and space counts. But as with all forms of writing, a little practice will soon alleviate any fears you may have.

Started in 2006 as a sort of extension of a few friends keeping each other updated as to what they were up to via SMS and with the first tweet ever sent being predictably "just setting up my twttr," Twitter is now one of the largest and most far-reaching social media platforms available. It's also very popular with writers, researchers, the media, and public commentators.

Twitter can be very liberating. What seems at first like a very restrictive form actually allows you to express yourself and your ideas extremely creatively. I find the trick is to throw the rule book away. Anything you learned about the English language at school—such as every sentence needing a subject, a verb, and an object—can be forgotten on Twitter. In a way, Twitter is a bit like a modern haiku—both strict and formulaic but also completely free and open to highly creative use of language. And of course, if you really do want to talk at length on a subject, you can just keep going over multiple consecutive postings in what is called a thread.

One of my favorite things about Twitter is how, if you set it up properly, it will have a life of its own—you can take your hands off the wheel, and the car will still keep going. Unlike your blog or your website, don't think of yourself as an author but as a curator. Sure, you are providing interesting and original content, but you are also finding, collecting, and disseminating other people's content in keeping with the theme or topic you have chosen for your Twitter account.

All you need to get active on Twitter is a photo of yourself (or a logo or even something else, if you are shy or want to remain anonymous), a panoramic photo for your backdrop, a catchy little name, and a micro manifesto. Once you've come up with that and have allowed Twitter to do all the verification and setup, you'll be ready to go. It really should take you no longer than five minutes.

Then start tweeting. You'll hear me say this again and again: writing online should be "little and often." Frequency is very important if you want to build and retain followers. Not only should your content be dynamic and interesting, but it should have an eye to keeping your audience coming back for more.

As with all online forms, variety is the key. Don't be afraid to insert images, post links, respond to things in the news, or retweet others' ideas. Never feel you have to sit down and come up with 280 characters of mind-shattering genius all on your own again and again and again. That's impossible. In fact—here's a little trick that makes it all so much easier—put a folder on your desktop, and whenever you see something interesting, copy it and paste it into your folder. Then, when you need to tweet and can't come up with anything original, just open this folder, and take inspiration from something you've saved. It's like putting ideas away for a rainy day.

And as with everything you are going to do online, there's very little point tweeting to yourself—you need an audience. Building up followers isn't actually that hard and bears out something I have noticed for quite some time now—we are all actually much nicer and more polite to each other online than we are offline. Online, if you link to someone, follow them, or befriend them, chances are they'll reciprocate before you know it. Of course, there are more than a few trolls and outright nuts out there, especially if you are working in what they might consider a controversial area, but don't be tempted to see their ravings as a sad cry for help—just block them and move on. Life's too short!

Once you have set up your Twitter account, start searching for like-minded souls. Put all your keywords into the search box, and see which accounts come up, then follow any you like. Twitter's algorithms will also suggest people you can follow based on your interests and search history. Hashtags are also a good thing to go searching for. An even shorter version of the "six words that sum up your expertise" exercise, they will lead you to some very interesting people worth connecting to. Soon, you'll be the curator of a one-stop shop for all things to do with your area of expertise. In fact, the real skill lies in resisting all the puppy and kitten pics you'll get distracted by and not following those accounts. Stay strong! Keep your account pure!

As with all communication, give some thought to your audience. In all probability, your Twitter followers are going to be looking at your account on their phones, probably while they're doing something else—travelling to work, having a coffee, or sitting at the back of the lecture theater where they think they can't be seen. They have limited time and possibly an even more limited attention span, so get to the point!

Your readers aren't always looking for extended words of deep wisdom—they want clever, funny, pithy, and to the point. They don't mind a bit of politics, so feel free to agitate and activate your audience if you have a cause and they can cope with an intelligent challenge to their ways of thinking (and keeping in mind your university's policies on public comment, of course). And Twitter can be fast—very, very fast. If you want to get the word out, get a movement started, or effect change, there is no place that is more like online wildfire than Twitter. British comedian Ricky Gervais had some very interesting thoughts on how this has changed animal rights activism in his Netflix special *Humanity*.

18
BLOGGING

Part diary, part confessional, part creative
writing exercise, and part promotional flyer,
a good blog should be addictive and have
your readers coming back for more.

As we move from Twitter to blogging, we're now moving up from a few hundred characters to a few hundred words. Essentially, we are in the area of midlength writing, and these principles apply to professional Facebook pages or articles you post in your LinkedIn profile too.

Before you begin, I'd recommend you ask yourself a few questions:

1. What is your purpose? Why are you blogging?
2. What kind of blog do you want to put together? Is it strictly work- or research-related, or do you want to be known as a public intellectual or commentator? Or is it a mix of these?
3. Who is your audience, and what are they looking for? Where do they go looking for information?

Once you've answered these questions, then reality-check your answers. Is blogging the best way to get your message across? And is a blog where your readership is looking for information? Let's say you are blogging to encourage a love of science, you want to combine research with enthusiastic commentary, and your audience is high school students whom you want to influence to study science in school and beyond. Ask yourself: Is a blog really the best way to spread that message? Do the students I want to reach read blogs? Could leaflets, a full website, or a scientists-in-schools program achieve the same result or better?

A blog can be attributed and quite personal; you can name it and take ownership of it. Or you can create a catchy name for yourself (more on this later). Alternatively, if you don't want to go solo, you can consider a collaborative or multiauthored blog. Sometimes an institution will have a corporate blog that is administered by a single person but written by all the members of a research team. Any or all of these options are perfectly fine, but you need to make these decisions before you set up your blog.

NAMING AND BRANDING

What will you name your blog? Does the name you've chosen mean something? There's no point in coming up with a clever-sounding name if it doesn't actually mean anything. You want it to resonate and stay in people's memories. And ideally, the name should relate to your content and match the names of any other online presence you might have. Look at space archaeologist Alice Gorman, otherwise known as Dr. Space Junk; Alice blogs as Dr. Space Junk, she tweets as @drspacejunk, and she is the proud author of the book *Dr Space Junk vs The Universe*. Perfect! Inger Mewburn, a.k.a. the Thesis Whisperer, is another great example. And if your name includes the sorts of keywords that might be put into Google by people looking for someone like you, then it's going to help with search engine optimization (SEO). Remember googleability.

And of course, as well as relating to the brand you are trying to promote and actually meaning something, your name should be memorable and intriguing. I remember doing an exercise with a group of scientists in Singapore, and a dermatologist came up with the name That Skin Guy. Not *The* Skin Guy, but *That* Skin Guy, with a subtle and clever hint of familiarity about it. It goes without saying that you should make sure you own the name before pursuing its use.

And finally, is your name flexible enough to be future-proofed? People change. Jobs change. Specializations change. If you brand yourself too specifically and then your career evolves and develops, you might find yourself with a digital presence that is meaningless for your next professional incarnation.

BLOGGING ESSENTIALS

Before you start, think about what you can and can't blog or comment on. What authority or expertise do you have, or at least do you want to be known for? And are you treading on any academic toes? I think it's best to go into these things with eyes wide open.

How often should you blog? The answer, as with all social media, is regularly. You want your audience to develop a routine and keep coming back to your blog to see if there's anything new. This is especially true if something happens that is relevant to you and your work; your audience will expect you to comment and will come looking to see what you've said. Don't disappoint them.

A blog post should only be a few hundred words at most. If you've really got more to say than that, split it into two or more posts, finishing each section with a bit of a cliffhanger. Not only will you get more bang for your buck with the same information, but you'll build an audience you are training to come back for more.

As with Twitter, setting up your blog should be the easiest thing you do all day, and the software will pretty much do it for you. Software comes and goes; at the moment, WordPress is the go-to platform. Unless you want to do something very complex, there is enough free software out there that you shouldn't have to pay a cent for this.

What should your blog look like? The trick, I think, is to keep it simple. Simplicity usually equates to elegance, which is not a bad thing to be known for online. Just use a simple color scheme and stay well away from overly fancy or complicated graphics and design schemes.

One thing you will find in most blogging software templates is a comments section. You probably should put some thought into whether you are going to interact with your readers and, if you are, how you will handle it. Personally, comments are the first thing I switch off whenever I set up a new website, but you might want to be more inclusive than me. Comments can allow you to create a sense of community and involvement for readers, which might encourage them to keep coming back for more. On the other hand, not every comment you receive is necessarily welcome or, it must be said, sane! And then there's the problem of trolling. The answer probably lies not so much in stifling free speech but rather keeping a careful lid on it by moderating and approving comments before they appear.

CONTENT AND CONNECTIONS

Blogging itself is fairly painless. First, stockpile content—always be on the lookout for ideas, information, data, pictures, charts, headlines, even jokes. Save them somewhere, and when you need content and inspiration fails to strike, just open your "Blog Ideas" folder and pull something out and away you go. Next, sketch out your post very quickly—a few bullet points will do. Then, as quickly as you can, write your first draft. You're not looking for accuracy or beautiful writing; you just want to get something down. Which leads to the next step: edit, then edit, then edit some more, and turn your hastily scribbled draft into beautiful writing. Finally, look over what you've written in terms of reach, readability, scannability, and, dare I say it, even a touch of clickbait. It looks good, it sounds good, but does it catch the eye? Will Google like it?

Tagging is probably the best route to visibility with your blog. Tags are little one- to three-word descriptions of your content that can be picked up in searches. Make sure that they are clear, that tags for the same piece don't repeat each other, and that they are not overly complicated. If you are unsure which keywords are best, there are plenty of online "keyword explorer" tools that will show you how your words rank. There are also plenty of websites that will help your SEO and have you rising through the ranks on Google.

It's all well and good coming up with exciting content, but if no one knows about it, then no one will read it. I always say it's a bit like having the world's best brochures designed and printed but then leaving them in boxes in the garage. So as we discussed with Twitter, get out there, make contact with like-minded individuals, link to each other, support each other, and become part of the online community. Never be shy or afraid to promote yourself.

And don't worry if you don't think you have enough time to blog. Trust me: you do. Blogging doesn't need to be an activity in its own right; it can quite easily be an extension or by-product of everything else you do, making it as close to effortless as you can get. You could, for example, use a version of a lecture or talk you've already given—either text or the graphic elements. You could throw out a question to your readers and then blog with their responses. Or it could be something as simple as a diary of your research or work. Don't make it any harder than it needs to be.

19
WEBSITES

If you see yourself as a brand, then your website is the center of your digital empire. It's the online equivalent of your brick-and-mortar flagship store.

Your website is a bit like your brochure of old. It's where you display samples of your wares, advertise your services, provide background information, and tell your life story—or at least the parts that you want made public. It makes a great "front door" to your digital presence and social media content (Twitter, Instagram, blog, and so on). You can carry out business through a website—it makes a great place to sell self-published writing, for example. You can embed content by including YouTube or Vimeo accounts, link your tweets, and so on. Really, it's a bit of a blank slate, and with a bit of imagination and a tiny bit of technical know-how, it can be anything you want it to be.

WEBSITE ESSENTIALS

So how do you set up a website? As always, your first step is to come up with a name. Your own name is often your best bet: it relates directly to you and everything you stand for. It's also particularly useful if you have a number of strings to your bow and, to mix a metaphor, need an umbrella under which to gather all the disparate elements of your professional life. I always have several different projects on the go at any given time, so simonclews.com is by far the easiest place to corral them. Otherwise, you can choose a website name that sums up you, your life, your expertise, your brand, your everything. It should be clever, witty, and, above all, catchy and memorable. And it has to be a name that is still available—you may need to get creative to claim your spot on the World Wide Web.

Once you've got the name sorted and you have claimed and registered it, you'll need to find someone to host it for you. Shop around. It's quite a fluid market, and there are always special deals on offer somewhere if you look hard enough. Registration and hosting will cost you a little bit, but these costs shouldn't be huge, and they are tax-deductible expenses if you use them for self-promotion or to conduct your business. Just ask your accountant about that.

And lastly, you need to design the site itself. Again—as with Twitter and blogging—the beauty of today's websites is that for the most part, they are template-driven. You look at a catalogue of thousands of predesigned sites, choose one that looks right for you, and then customize it. I remember a time when, if you wanted to design a website, you had to be a graphic designer and software programmer all rolled into one, and even then, the results were fairly basic. Now you go to something like WordPress, and you'll find some astonishingly well-designed sites on offer and plug-ins that will allow you to include all sorts of automated processes and even sell your wares online.

SITE DESIGN AND FEATURES

I think we should be aiming to design simple, classic, tasteful, and timeless websites. I'd suggest you come up with your own "house style" and stick to it. If you have a logo or an image that you like to use, find yourself a free online color-palette generator, and let it choose two or three colors based on your graphic, then stick with those as your color scheme. The same with fonts. All you need are a couple that look good together and a few variants on each—bold, italic, and so on—but no more. But most templates will deal with all this for you, just leaving you to come up with the winning content.

While websites can be highly creative, they also often observe some quite traditional conventions. You will usually find headings like "About" or "Contact," for example, often in similar places on the page.

There is a lot of research into how people look at web pages. It seems the vast majority of us look at a web page by following the shape of a letter F—that is, we look along the top, across the middle, and down the left-hand side. That doesn't mean we don't look at the rest of the page, but we do so only after following the F-shape convention. If you visit one of the successful, high-profile online retailers like Amazon or eBay, look at what is in these spots on the page. Invariably, that's what they want you to look at and click on.

As a general rule, we don't like to scroll endlessly down a very long page. This is becoming increasingly relevant as we look at websites more on our phones than on other devices. So think about links to separate pages, with each one detailing a different part of your story, rather than one long page with everything on it. And while we're on the subject of phones, when you have finished your page and are testing it, always preview it on a phone—this is where the majority of people will look at it.

Once your website is up and running, it can stay there until you need to change it. Unlike other forms of online writing where half the point is to encourage repeat visitation to check out new content, a website is fairly static. Sure, refresh the look from time to time, but don't feel pressured to come up with something new every single day—save that for a blog or Twitter. And if you have embedded that blog or your YouTube channel or Twitter feed into your website, then the site will have new content all the time anyway.

20

WORKING WITH THE MEDIA

There are plenty of places where your expertise will get to shine, but the acid test of a real "expert" is how well they can work with the media.

N ow that you have set up your own digital empire, I think it's time to start interacting with the rest of the world, starting by working with the media. It's one of the most important things you will do as an "expert." So if being an expert involves working with the media, let's see just how ready you are to work with them, shall we? Let me ask you a few simple questions:

- What's the lead story in your local daily newspaper today? Print or online will do.
- Who does the drive-time slot on your local talk radio station these days?
- What news (either online or offline) did you read this morning?
- Who's your favorite print media journalist?
- Who's your favorite radio or TV media personality?

- What, in your opinion, is the best website for news?
- Do you subscribe to any journals, magazines, newspapers, or websites to keep up with the news?

If any of those questions stumped you, you probably need to become more media-savvy. Not only do you need to know what's going on in the world to see the context within which your work sits, but you can't really deal with the media if you don't know them well.

We've already tested your media friendliness. Remember imagining you're going to appear on radio or television to give some expert commentary on a news development in your field? Make sure you can finish the sentence "And after this break, we'll be meeting..." in somewhere between six and ten words. And don't forget this is for a TV or radio audience who know nothing about you and probably only have a passing understanding of the field you work in.

And one last test: What news alerts service do you use? Now, if you have an answer to this question, well done. But if you're scratching your head and wondering what I am talking about, allow me to change your life for the better. Lots of search engines offer news alerts. You simply put keywords into the system, and every morning (or whenever you tell it to), you'll receive a summary of what has been happening in the world that features your topics of interest. Not only will you stay abreast of relevant current affairs, but if you need inspiration or source material for things like tweeting or blogging, this is by far the easiest way to get it.

CONNECTING WITH MEDIA

There are many reasons why you might need the media. At the start of the research process, you might need supporters or participants;

along the way, it never hurts to show those who have funded you what you are doing; and at the end, media mentions of your results are often the impetus for the next lot of funding to take you into the next stage in the research. And so it starts all over again.

And the media need you. Across all the different channels—print, radio, TV, and digital—people are always looking for experts: those who have a public profile and a degree of expertise in a particular field. As we talked about earlier, the media don't care if you're not the most qualified person in that field. Remember the rule: if you imagine a room full of people, the person who knows more than anyone else in the room is the expert. I heard someone talking about bushfires on the radio the other day. He was actually quite good on-air talent, but he shot himself in the foot by starting the interview by making a huge deal out of the fact that he was a fire ecologist, not a fire behaviorist. You could almost hear a collective "WTF?!" from the listeners.

All universities have a media office of some sort. It might be called the media office, or it might go by some other name—external relations, marketing and communications, or something like that. But essentially they all do the same thing—they attempt to get as much positive coverage in the media as they can about the university. Generally, they will be staffed by people with experience in marketing and publicity and will often have an old journalist or two on staff. Mostly they know what they are talking about. The real problem, however, is that there is rarely more than a handful of people working in them, and there are thousands of people on staff and in the student population, all of whom would love to be featured in the media. And unless someone really has come up with a cure for cancer, the media office priorities are, in order, one, the university, two, the boss (the president, vice chancellor, or whatever fancy title your university gives its chief academic officer), and three, everyone else. So it can be very useful to learn to fend for yourself when dealing with the media, although you can ask your media office if they can help you with media training or feature you on their "find an expert" web page if they have one. Both are good ways of getting noticed without asking too much of them.

Very importantly, even in the digital age, working with the media is all about connecting with people and cultivating relationships. Editors like to get to know the people they are working with, and similarly writers like to feel supported, even nurtured by a good editor. When it works well, a good writer-editor relationship can be of great mutual benefit.

Always do some research on the media you are dealing with, as you can be certain they will have done their research on you. Who is their audience? What sorts of stories or angles might appeal to them? That sort of thing. Get to know them.

Think about offering something different and memorable too. The chances are you won't be the only person getting in touch with a publication and pitching a story to them that day. If you are working in an area that has topicality or newsworthiness, you definitely won't be the only person pitching a story on that subject either. So your point of difference can be quite crucial in getting past the gatekeeper and attracting their interest. Always ask yourself: What do I know that no one else does? What connection to the story do I have that can't be replicated by anyone else?

The business side of your relationship with the media is also important. They are looking for people who are reliable and trustworthy, who will deliver what they promise, and, as a result, who will help them do their jobs. They want writers who understand the sacrosanct nature of word counts and deadlines, and they want on-air talent who can pronounce difficult words and unfamiliar names with absolute fluency. If you look at this as a business transaction, you need to think how you can best meet the needs of your clients.

STRATEGIES FOR WORKING WITH MEDIA

When working with the media, it's very important that you plan ahead. You will be dealing with busy and probably overworked people who don't have time to wait while you sit and have a bit of a think. You also need more than ever before to start thinking in bite-sized pieces; often your entire research project will end up as a minute or less of airtime, so you need to be able to get to the point as soon as you open your mouth or put pen to paper.

If you are part of a research team, decide on a dedicated media spokesperson; this is not necessarily the person who is most qualified to talk about the research but rather the person who is going to look good and sound confident on camera or mic. The story comes first. In fact, you can take this a step further and consider engaging a professional to train your spokesperson. In extreme circumstances, you might pay someone to speak for you, but this is a last resort; you'd need to spend quite a bit of time (and money) briefing them. The science communication crowd is ahead of the game in offering media training; maybe see if you can find a local organization and talk to them.

Dealing with the media is like any other activity where you try to get your voice heard in the outside world—it can be a bit hit-and-miss. It can often take time to break through, so be persistent and patient, and above all, don't take rejection personally—it just happens. There's an awful lot of "noise" these days, and being heard above it isn't a given, no matter how earth-shattering your discoveries are. As a general rule, always make sure you are active, ideally a bit proactive. Nothing in life—especially the attention of the media—comes to those who wait. If it does, chances are you're in the spotlight for all the wrong reasons! Keep your eyes open for opportunities wherever you go, and think two or even three steps ahead. Work the system, and make the best use of your connections (and their connections too).

MEDIA RELEASES

Media releases (originally called press releases) have been around for-ever and are still the best way to make initial written contact with the media. Right now, you might simply be helping your media office with a few facts and figures as they put one together for you, but at some point in your career, you may well be called on to do this.

First, ask yourself: What is the main point of my story? You really should be able to answer this in a dozen or so words. Think how your story might be introduced on the news. In fact, what you write could end up being exactly what they use on the news. Ask yourself: Is my story really interesting, and if so, why? Really challenge yourself on this one. When we say "interesting," remember we mean to other people—not you, not your team, and not people in your field. It's very easy to make the leap from "I think this is fascinating" to "Surely everyone else will think it is fascinating too," when in reality, this is far from the truth.

Geographic reach is very important for the media—they all work in specific markets and rarely stray outside their boundaries. A local paper, for example, will be reluctant to take stories that are set in suburbs on the other side of town. So is your audience local, regional, state, or national? Is your story of global importance? Of course, the same story can be recast for whatever territory the particular media you are contacting operates in. I have seen the same story go from a very local "Iowa girl makes good" approach to having a national "top American scientist makes major advance" angle—the same story, just slightly rewritten.

What's your angle? What's your take on the story in question? The more unusual or more interesting the angle of your story, the more likely it is that the media will be interested.

Once you have the content sorted, you need to think about which media organizations you will target. Think carefully about what your message is and who is most likely to be interested in it. Remember: not everyone is interested in everything!

Then think about writing your story. As you do this, remember that with any story, everyone, including the media, always wants to know: Who? What? Where? When? Why? How? These questions—often called "the five Ws and an H" that feature on the first day of almost every journalism course—form the skeleton of every story. They are the glue that holds it together.

Always think visual too—we live in a very visual world now. If you have a photo opportunity related to your story, you're ahead of the game. If you don't, think of creating one. Use your imagination. As an exercise, think about writing a media release for a news item based on your research. There are some serious dos and don'ts you need to consider.

The Dos

- Keep it short. One page is ideal, and a second page may not even get read.

- Keep it simple. Busy journalists want the information quickly and easily; they can call for more details if they need them.
- Be objective.
- Proofread it for spelling and grammatical errors (which means more than just spellchecking it on the computer), and then get someone else to read it.
- Include contact details (name, email address, and telephone numbers) at the end of the release.
- Remember to date the release. If the media can't quickly see if the story is topical or not, they'll move on to one that is.

The Don'ts

- Don't get anything wrong. Fact-check everything.
- Don't exaggerate.
- Don't put too many ideas into one sentence.
- Don't waffle.

Here are the elements of a typical media release. It will probably only exist digitally, but it will still need to appear on your letterhead with all your contact details included.

MEDIA RELEASE

For immediate release: [date]
or
Embargoed until: [time/date]

(really try to grab their attention with this, make your story stand out) ⟶ **Headline**

Photo Opportunity ⟵ (What it is, where it is, when it is and contact details)

Paragraph 1: Summarize the story—who, what, where, when, and why? And how, of course.

Paragraph 2: Put in more details to flesh out your story.

Paragraph 3: "Quotes from experts involved in the story." Ideally each quote should make one point.

Paragraph 4: Extra relevant information.

(No idea why they put that there, but they do. Same as "The End" at the end of a film. Is it not obvious?)

<ENDS> ⟵

If you feel compelled to add extra details, make sure they are on a second page. If the media outlet decides to follow up your story, the journalist who gets the assignment might look at them. Call them something like "Notes for Editors" and provide background information, definitions, and any additional relevant information or facts and figures, and outline what you have to offer in the way of potential interviewees (do you have a patient who has recovered because of your wonder drug or a farmer whose crop has doubled thanks to your new strain of wheat?). But keep it short.

Make sure you supply contact numbers where you can be reached day or night—not the administrative assistant's office number, for example. I cannot emphasize enough that you need to be reachable. The media will call you once, but if they have to chase you down, they are unlikely to call again. I have seen so many good stories fall by the wayside because someone has put their office number on the release and then promptly gone away for the weekend or included their cell number but left their phone on silent at home. Media people don't like being frustrated. And they have long memories.

Of course, writing a media release is only half the equation; what you do with it and how you distribute it is what will really make it work. This is another area your media office should be able to help you with. There are media directories and listings available—online and in hard copy—that you will need so you can decide where to send your release. Make sure the publications you are targeting are appropriate—in terms of subject matter and geographic reach—as to do otherwise risks wasting both the media outlet's time and your own.

Once you have sent your media release out, you need to follow up. The timing of this is crucial, as you don't want to pester, but equally you don't want to be overlooked. I'd give them at least a few hours, and if your story can wait overnight, it's probably best to contact them the next day. Send a short, polite "I'm just following up on a release I sent yesterday" sort of message, and if you don't get a reply to that, assume you're never going to get one.

INTERVIEW TIPS

Now, let's be optimistic and look at what happens when the media bites and wants to talk to you.

Timing. If the interview is to be face-to-face, organize a time to meet that is convenient for both you and the journalist. It's important not to feel rushed or pressured so that you are 100 percent ready to answer their questions when you meet. Why not have a brief chat on the phone beforehand and then meet in person when you are good and ready? The same applies if you intend to meet online.

Preparation. Get your team together before the media person arrives and double-check what message you want to get across. Make sure it's clear and consistent. And if you've promised the journalist anything on the day, like an experiment to photograph or the latest results to take away, have it all ready to go well before the meeting.

No question should come as a surprise to you. You know your topic, and you know the media you are dealing with. Just think laterally; think through what you are going to say and then anticipate their questions and your answers. It shouldn't be hard. Once you've figured out all the questions, come up with all the answers. No surprises, right?

Appearance. Make sure you look your best, especially if you are appearing on camera—you don't want a disheveled scientist or a messy lab. If the television cameras are coming or if you're appearing via Zoom or Skype, don't wear stripes (they do a weird thing called strobing on camera). Avoid any noisy jewelry like bangles or metallic necklaces. Don't wear synthetic garments that might build up static. If you're going for that "executive stubble" look, make sure it's tidy and doesn't look like you slept in and forgot to shave. A light touch with the makeup brush will counteract the harsh, portable light (often called a "sun gun") they might bring with them. And give your hair a once-over with the brush—after all, you want to be remembered for your research, not your bad hair.

Speaking and listening. Listen very carefully to the journalist's questions, and answer them as succinctly as possible. Don't guess or make up anything. It's perfectly acceptable to say that you will have to get back to them later with a particular detail you don't currently have to hand. And always, always, *always* remember that there is no such thing as "off the record" and all microphones are *always* on! We've all heard stories of politicians and celebrities caught saying awful things when they thought they were off mic. Don't let this happen to you.

Avoid "er" and "um"; try not to start your sentences with "so" (very academic) or "look" (both defensive *and* confrontational); and don't say anything that makes you sound like an academic. The "distribution of resources to confer tectonic supremacies of words and perspective" is not going to help you make the front page, I'm afraid.

Humor. If you don't have a sense of humor, can I suggest you find someone else who does? It is entirely possible that the media might make light of your story—they won't openly attack you, but they are often looking for the funny side of things. Certainly, they want you to be bright and breezy and able to take a joke. So don't take yourself too seriously, and if your interviewer says something that is supposed to be funny, just smile—even if it isn't. And never tell them their question is stupid. Even if it is.

Practice. Someone who is "good talent" will always have some apparently spontaneous but well-rehearsed anecdotes handy. If you're really good, you'll be able to trot these out again and again and again and make each time sound like it's the first time you've told that story. In fact, as odd as this sounds, you can actually practice speaking "off the cuff."

BUILDING MEDIA RELATIONSHIPS

Being nice to the media is a very nice thing to do. It helps build those all-important relationships that will give you a leg up next time you need a little attention. Be polite and always call the journalist yourself; certainly don't get your assistant to call, or someone who has no idea about the story pitch. It's just time-wasting and insulting. Don't be a pest on the phone, and don't hassle journalists with multiple phone calls. And if you have to leave a message, always say what you're calling about. Coyness will get you nowhere.

Once you have been interviewed, don't ask for copies of the story. And don't assume you're going to get approval or sign-off on the story. In fact, sometimes deadlines move so fast that journalists can't even tell you when the piece they are writing is going to be published, and you only find out you're in the papers because a friend tells you they've just read about you. It happens.

Never miss a deadline. If someone asks you to send them additional material by a particular time, they are doing it because they also have a looming deadline. If you don't send it in, don't assume they will chase you. Often, they don't have time to do this and will simply move on to a story where the person involved has sent through the background material they need.

And if your story gets cut or edited in a way you don't like, just bite your lip, sit on your hands, and grin and bear it. If there's a factual error, just let them know politely; otherwise, don't worry about it—you're still in the news, after all.

It's all about building up positive relationships; media people are *people* too. Have you ever contacted a journalist to say you liked a story they wrote? Or if they wrote about you or your research, did you thank them and give them feedback? Why not offer them first right of refusal on future stories and stay in touch? And pass their names and contact details on to your colleagues; being a source of interesting stories for them will only enhance your status as a go-to person.

21

NEWSPAPERS AND MAGAZINES

Often your first port of call as an engaged researcher, newspapers and magazines (print and online) are where you will reach audiences in numbers you've only dreamed of before now.

There are conceivably three areas—news, opinion, and features—where you could write for newspapers and magazines, although in reality, you're probably only going to get to have a go at two of them. There is a nice chronology to this process—something happens (news), someone comments on it soon after (opinion), and then later on, with the luxury of time and hindsight, someone reflects on it (features). The twenty-four-hour news cycle is having some effect on this, but mostly only to make the process faster.

Let's start with the news. We all know what the news is. Something happens in the world, and it needs to be reported on. For the most part, this reporting is done by journalists. Of course, like pretty much everything else, the digital revolution is changing all that. Anyone with a phone and an internet connection these days can call themselves a "citizen journalist," although without editorial gatekeeping, high-quality journalism is not necessarily guaranteed.

OPINION PIECES

The opinion pages are almost certainly where you will make your debut in print. This part of the newspaper is often referred to as the "op eds." I used to think "op" had something to do with opinion. It wasn't until embarrassingly recently that I found out that in a traditional newspaper, you used to have the editorial page on one side of the tabloid foldout, which meant the facing page was "opposite the editorial" page, often abbreviated to "op ed."

Opinion can be both active and reactive. Often something has happened in the world that requires expert commentary. This is where you come in. You can explain the background to a situation, the science behind it, the history or the ethics of it. You can help us understand the wider ramifications and repercussions. Sometimes you might be more proactive—you will see some injustice or an issue that needs challenging and use the opinion pages to issue a rallying cry or a call for action. You'll probably have somewhere between four hundred and eight hundred words to play with.

Before you can write your piece, you need to know who you are writing for, both the publication and its readership. Just as every audience is unique, so too every news outlet you could write for has its own house style, areas it favors, political positions it supports, and a very specific audience. So if you want to write for a newspaper, whether it be the *New York Times*, the *Guardian*, or the *Sydney Morning Herald*, the first thing you need to do (if you aren't doing this already) is read it. You'll get a feel for the publication and the sorts of stories they are running and avoid that embarrassing situation of pitching a story on a topical issue only to be told "Yes, we are interested in that issue—so interested, in fact, that we ran a story just like yours yesterday." Not a good look.

Then you must be either one, timely and newsy or two, able to somehow create the news—or at least stir up a bit of a public discussion and create a talking point. The former is much easier to do and is how the majority of opinion pieces come into being. This is also an area where your online news alerts really come into their own. You wake up, open your email, find out that something major has happened in the world that impacts on your research area; then you quickly knock out a pitch, send it in, and before you've even finished your first coffee, you might have a newspaper interested in your story. Not a bad way to start the day.

So once we've identified those approaches, how do we write a good opinion piece?

This shouldn't really need to be said, but to pitch an opinion piece, you need to **have a strong opinion**. I always suggest you try thumping your desk with your fist and finishing the sentence "I firmly believe that..." If you can't finish this sentence, you may still have a good idea for a piece of writing, but you probably don't have an opinion piece.

It also really helps if you **have a strong personal link** to your story. Knowing more than the rest of us will ensure your writing is intelligent and informed, but caring more will make it really special. It will also help with the all-important point of difference that everyone is looking for when pitching a story. Maybe you were there when the incident happened. Maybe you know or, better still, are related to a character in the drama that has unfolded. Anything that puts you closer to the center of the action is good. Sometimes this might seem unclear at first, but when it is, I always ask the researcher to think back to the time when they chose their topic. You'd be surprised how many people choose their specializations based on, or even inspired by, things that happen in their personal lives.

With your opinion pieces, **tell us something new**; don't tell us what we already know. Your job is not to report the news. If you are commenting on a current event, you can assume that we already know a lot about the story, and even with historic events, it's probably best to go easy on the exposition. We will have been bombarded with nonstop news on our televisions, computer screens, and phones ever since the news broke. Your job is to help us make sense of this barrage of information and to put it into some sort of perspective or context.

Wherever possible, **take an interesting and different angle** from the rest of the world. Never be obvious; never give us what we are expecting to read. Surprise us if you can. Not only will this capture the attention of your readers and fire up their imaginations, but it will get you to the head of the line in the pitching process. The reality is that, especially if you are working with highly topical stories, you won't be the only person pitching a story on that subject. I like to use what I call the "rule of ninety-nine others." Whatever you want to do in life—get a grant, secure a job, get your story published—so do ninety-nine others, and they are just as smart, connected, and informed as you. So you have to get ahead of the pack.

Get to the point. You only have a few hundred words to play with, so you can't ramble, waffle, or otherwise digress. And you certainly can't repeat yourself. Just get on with it!

Opinion pieces are quite traditional and formulaic, so you need to **understand their structure**. One option for structuring your piece is the "OREO" approach:

- Opinion (What do you think?)
- Reasons (Why do you think this?)

- Examples (Can you illustrate your reasons?)
- Opinion (What do you think again?)

Generally speaking, a winning opinion piece focuses on one issue or idea, gets to the point, and keeps it short and sweet. It will have a killer opening line that will grab the reader's attention and propel them to keep reading. This, of course, will be followed by an equally impressive opening paragraph, and the piece will end with a killer closing line. It may use a circular structure whereby it starts in one place, heads off to discuss a number of different facets of the topic, and ends up where it started, drawing the piece to a conclusion in a very satisfying and rewarding way for the reader.

You can **make your piece controversial** (which helps sell newspapers), but not outrageously so. Unless you want a regular column in the pages of a tabloid paper, of course, in which case just go ahead and ensure it's as outrageous and offensive as possible.

Be personal and conversational in your opinion piece. You can even be humorous, if you can make that work. A light touch often makes difficult issues easier to deal with and can get through to resistant readers. But if humor is not something you are comfortable with—and not everyone is—don't attempt it. Just stick with what you are good at.

Express your opinion clearly and firmly. Your reader shouldn't be left in any doubt as to what you think. Educate your reader, and provide them with some insight, but avoid the temptation to preach. You want to convince them with facts and logic, not by haranguing them from some imaginary soapbox.

Avoid introspection and navel-gazing. By all means, work through the inner turmoil that led you to your position, but don't waste words telling us about it. And never offer an opinion on an opinion or seek a right of reply. Academic journals are full of petty feuds that seem to last for years, whereas the world of commercial media just wants a strong, well-written opinion piece that gets read, talked about, hotly debated even, and then is moved aside for the next big issue.

FEATURES

Once you've written a few opinion pieces (assuming you have a bit of a public profile and a distinct digital footprint), you will probably move on to writing a few feature pieces. A feature is a longer piece— usually one thousand to fifteen hundred words for a short article and two thousand to three thousand for a longer piece—that can be found in standalone magazines or the weekend supplements of daily newspapers or their online equivalents.

Features are very similar to opinion pieces but also very different. One of the key differences will be in timeliness or topicality. Opinion is invariably based on current events and is newsy and topical. Features usually add the dimensions of time and distance to allow a bit of reflection and analysis to be factored into the mix. However, while they aren't overtly timely or topical, readers (and, importantly, publications) quite like them to appear to be so. Feature stories often open with some sort of fabricated contemporaneity—"a hundred years to the day since...," "on the eve of the announcement of...," or "as we approach the anniversary of the signing of the...." That sort of thing.

As with your opinion pieces, it helps to have a personal connection. And we don't want you to tell us things we already know; if the story is about something recent, the twenty-four-hour news coverage will still be in our heads, and if it isn't, we will have had plenty of time to come across the facts and process them.

You will have a bit more room to maneuver, however, so you can focus on a couple of big issues if you like, three if you're really good, but probably not many more. Don't try to cram too much in. It just ends up confusing and ultimately overwhelming your readers. Now here's a big difference; if your opinion piece began life with your banging your fist on the table and loudly proclaiming, "I firmly think that...," your feature may well start with, "Once upon a time..." That's right; we want you to tell us a story. And it's a story with nuanced characters that you bring to life and make three-dimensional and believable. Give your characters dialogue—go talk to people involved in the original news item, and quote them or use anecdotes—and have a protagonist, even an antagonist if there's conflict. Forget academic articles; instead think books, plays, and movies and the sorts of narratives that drive them.

The rules of being personal and chatty, even humorous if you can, and not trying to ram ideas down your readers' throats apply as much to features as they do to opinion pieces. And think of possible visuals in case you're asked. You won't necessarily have to source them or get into that horrible maze that is rights and permissions, but someone may well ask you what they could use to liven up the look of your story.

PITCHING

OK, we've got one half of the equation in place. You've decided what you want to write for the print media, but how do you get your words into print? The answer is you pitch. So now I am going to help you make the perfect pitch.

At this point, we are entering into the *business* of writing. So for a moment, concentrate on the client-provider relationship, because as crass and commercial as that sounds, that's exactly what we are attempting to enter into when we pitch our work to a newspaper or a magazine.

We've already talked about this, but just to emphasize: if you are going to pitch a story to a particular publication, you have to read that publication to get to know them and to find out what sorts of stories they have published and might conceivably publish.

Then, assuming you like the publication and its readership and you are comfortable writing in the style they seem to be looking for, you next have to sell your wares. This is going to be in an email. And as you are dealing with busy people who may receive hundreds of similar emails a day, it needs to be a short, sharp email that doesn't waste any time getting to the point.

Your email should answer the question "Why?" in four different ways:

1. Why this story?
2. Why this publication?
3. Why now?
4. Why you?

And all this is answered implicitly, rather than explicitly, in a handful of carefully crafted short sentences sent by email to the editor of the section you want to be published in. Let's look at them one at a time.

Why this story? As an editor who could potentially publish your story, I could conceivably publish anything I wanted. There are no banned topics; nothing is off-limits. Even taboo topics are OK if they are handled sensitively. So why should I be interested in your story? Sell it to me!

Why this publication? Your story could run in any publication on the planet, so why should I publish your story in my newspaper? Convince me!

Why now? I could run any story at any time in my newspaper. Hell, I can do a Christmas feature slap-bang in the middle of July if I feel like it! So why is now the time to run your story? What makes it topical?

And then the last, but probably most important question of all: **Why you?** Any good journalist should be able to dive into the internet and come up with enough interesting stuff to throw together a few hundred words on your topic, so why should you be the one to write this piece? Of course, while this might sound like the hardest question, it is actually the easiest. The answer is that you know more, and you care more. You probably also have a unique perspective that makes you stand out from the competition. So don't be shy. Tell them why you're the best.

All this is packaged up into a nice little email: four to five sentences describing who you are, what you've done, and what you know and maybe six or seven sentences on how you plan to write the story, the angle you'll take, the tone you'll adopt. That sort of thing. That's somewhere in the vicinity of ten to twelve short, sharp, pithy sentences. No more.

And it shouldn't need to be said, but this email has to be beautifully written, grammatically correct, and spellchecked to within an inch of its life. It is, after all, the very first sample of your art, craft, and prowess as a writer that your potential client is going to see. No one is ever going to read an email and say: "Sure it's a half-assed, half-baked effort, but I bet she can write!" Even the subject header needs to be carefully thought out—in a way, it serves the same function as the headline of a story. It should attract the editor's eye amid a sea of other story ideas and make them want to pick yours out of the pile.

There's a sample of a pitch email in the appendices for you to have a look at.

Who you send this email to matters too. Newspapers and magazines are not homogenous entities but rather a series of pages or sections, each ruled over by an editor and brought together under the watchful eye of an editor in chief. So it's important that you send your pitch to the editor of the section you want to be in. It's a nice idea that if you don't do this and it ends up in the wrong inbox, someone will carefully forward it to the right person, but that's probably not going to happen. Your misdirected email will just disappear into some electronic void, never to be seen again.

And never make the mistake of assuming the science editor gets science, that the arts editor likes the arts, or the business editor understands facts, figures, and dollar signs. Sometimes they will, and often the longer they stay with a particular section, the more they get to like and understand it, but their primary skill is that of an editor. Which is why they make such good representatives for their readers and which is why you need to assume they know nothing and need to explain everything to them—just like a general readership.

Newspapers and magazines also tend to have fairly flat career structures, with people rotating within the various sections of the publication to stay sane and interested. So on the morning you intend to pitch, it's vital that you call the switchboard or check the publication's website to make sure you are pitching to the relevant editor on duty that day.

Then you press Send and wait. And wait.

And wait some more.

In an ideal world, they will get back to you, and these days, you are increasingly likely to receive some sort of automatic acknowledgment so at least you know your email didn't fall off the radar, but sometimes you hear nothing. So you need to follow up. I think how long you give them and when you follow up is probably best based on the frequency of publication. So a daily newspaper gets twenty-four hours, a weekly magazine gets seven days, and so on. I wouldn't wait longer than a month, so four weeks is probably the most you should give any publication. You follow up once, politely and succinctly: "Hi there. I pitched you an idea for a story yesterday about our work on the COVID-19 vaccine, and I wondered if you'd had a chance to look at it. I think it's an important issue, and I am keen to see it published. Please let me know if you're interested." And that's probably all you need to say. You might want to repeat the subject header you used for your email or even forward your original email so it's relatively easy for them to find, but you shouldn't need to add anything else. Really, they either want it or they don't. If you need to sell it to them any harder, they probably don't want it but are just being polite. And if they do want it, this little reminder will prompt them to get back to you.

But if this follow-up generates no response, or they tell you they are not interested in the topic, they have already commissioned someone else, or their pages are full, dust yourself off, get back up, and move on. Moving on can either mean moving on to the next story or tweaking this pitch and sending it to another publication for their consideration. Of course, if you're really clever, you will have already anticipated this and pitched three or more slightly different versions of the same story to three different publications. There's no rule that says you have to pitch to one publication at a time, and what's the worst thing that can happen? Two newspapers wanting to run your story! To use the phrase "bidding war" is probably an exaggeration, but how good would it be if you had to choose where you wanted your piece to run and then very gently let the losing party down—while keeping the door open for the next pitch?

Newspapers and magazines are very exciting places to share your research stories with large numbers of people. Get a few of these under your belt, and your platform will flourish. And the digital world, while slowly killing physical print media, is also addressing the short shelf life of print newspaper articles. These days, a well-written piece that people come back to read again and again will have an almost limitless life online. And to check that was true, I just put three words into Google, and the first result I got back was a piece I wrote more than five years ago about the fiftieth anniversary of the founding of the city-state of Singapore. Still up there. Still being read.

22

BOOKS

The rumors of their death have been greatly
exaggerated: books are very much alive and well
and are a perfectly viable and exciting format
in which to tell your research stories.

Despite every writers' festival I have ever been to featuring at least one session prophesying the death of the book, they are very much a thing and are still being bought and read all around the world in vast numbers. I was at a conference once and heard an astonishing statistic. I have no idea how this was calculated, but it came from an international publishers' organization, so I assume it had some basis in fact. The claim was that somewhere on this planet, a new book is published every three seconds. Every three seconds! If that's even half true, it's an astonishing number of books being churned out year after year. Certainly, the most recent UNESCO figures from 2013 have China pushing 440,000 and the States following with just over 300,000 titles a year. If my math is right, that's a new title every forty or so seconds from those two countries alone.

I probably should mention here that we are talking about what are called "trade" books. These are the sorts of titles that end up in bookstores or online booksellers' websites and that are bought and read by thousands of people. They are a commercial proposition where risks are taken by publishers in the hope of turning a profit. Niche scholarly titles, often subsidized in some way, with tiny print runs and sometimes hefty price tags, are a whole other ball game, and you'll be able to find plenty of advice on that front simply by asking around your department or faculty.

If you are interested in turning your work into a book, you need to ask yourself a few questions to begin with. What in your research do you think would make a book? Even though you have much more room to move than in a newspaper or magazine article and may well end up with a similar word count to a PhD thesis, not every aspect of your research is book-worthy. You also need to think about what sort of book you'd like to write. Books are very much like people—they are all individuals with their own personalities and quirks. So what is your book like? What is its style? Is it serious or funny? Is it text only or illustrated? Is it formal or more conversational? If you remember one of the first things we discussed, you'll recall that the answers to these first two questions will be determined by your response to the next question: Who is the audience for your book?

I quite like the exercise of imagining what your book might look like, closing your eyes, and holding this imaginary book in your hands. Turn it over, feel the weight and substance of it, and look at the beauty of it. Then fix that idea firmly in your head, and set it as your destination. Which brings us to the wonderful world of publishing.

23

TRADITIONAL PUBLISHING

A quick history lesson on the traditional route
books take from the "Hey, I've got a great
idea for a book!" stage to the "$29.95—
wow, that's a lot less than $30!" stage.

At some point in the mid-fifteenth century, Johannes Gutenberg first pressed Print, and the world changed overnight. And with the world's first print job (presumably swiftly followed by the world's first paper jam), the publishing industry was born. So traditional publishing, sometimes called legacy publishing, has been around for a very long time. To this day, it's still a perfectly viable option for you to get your ideas out to the big wide world—and an exciting and desirable one.

To start, ask yourself these questions: What do I hope to achieve by having a book published? What do I want a book to do for me? A book can be the road to many things—fame and fortune are the most obvious (and least likely!), but you might need a book as a calling card, for example. You might want to get on the speakers' circuit, in which case a book is a good way to show a sample of your wares and quickly establish some credibility. Or I've seen books function as what the music business calls "merch"—if you're already in the business of talking to groups, you may want something else to offer them. Again, a book is a great way to extend the reach of your message long after you've ridden off into the sunset. But whatever your aim is, make sure it's clear in your mind from the start. That way, you can think strategically along the way and deal with disappointment if it arises.

FINDING THE RIGHT PUBLISHER

The process begins with what sounds like a simple first step: the author pitches their idea for a book to a publisher. Of course, it helps tremendously if you pitch your book to the *right* publisher. No two publishers are alike, and for the writer-publisher relationship to work at its best, you really need to find the one that's right for you. Despite some of them offering a fairly corporate public face, once you look beyond their business plans and strategic directions, publishers are actually very human organizations, often shaped by the personal tastes and interests of their senior staff. I know of one publishing house that is widely renowned as one of the leading publishers of military history, for example. This is not because they've done market research into potential audiences or commissioned business planning that led them in this particular direction; it's simply because two of their key publishers absolutely love military history. They have a passion for it. Which is exactly what you are looking for. If someone believes in your work and can share your passion and excitement, odds are they're going to do a really good job creating and selling your book.

The nature and scale of the publishing house is also very important. Let me tell you a tale of two publishers. Imagine you have a good idea for a first book that is going to sell a respectable twenty-five hundred copies. If you go to a small independent publisher, they will be enthusiastic, they'll mentor you, they'll look after you, and they'll print, let's say, three thousand copies of your book. That means when all the accounts are in, you will have sold over 80 percent of your print run. That makes you a very successful author in their eyes, certainly someone with whom they'd like to chat about a second book. On the other hand, you could have ended up with a major multinational publisher that, while having more staff and resources to throw at you, will probably not be quite so nurturing. They'll print fifteen thousand copies of your book because they don't really do numbers lower than that. This scenario means you won't even sell 20 percent of your print run and, in their eyes, will look like a bit of a dud. You definitely shouldn't expect coffee and cake and a chat about your future relationship!

You also need to avoid that black hole of publishing: the slush pile. A small number of publishers will accept what are called unsolicited manuscripts—anything that a publisher hasn't actively invited or personally sought out—and if you submit your book proposal in this way, make sure you observe their submission conditions to the letter. But books that arrive uninvited in the mail are often placed unceremoniously in a big pile to languish, gather dust, and generally wait a very long time before someone gets around to reading them. That's the slush pile. No author wants their book to end up there. As a rule, the person whose job it is to sift through this pile will be fairly low down in the organizational food chain and could even be a work experience student or an intern. Just to put all this in perspective, I once heard the person who had been rostered on to wade through the slush pile in a major publishing house referred to as the "poison taster." Sad but true.

There is a really good exercise you can do to help you find the right publisher. Go into a bookstore (you can do this online, but it's not quite the same), and look for your book. That's right—look for the book you have yet to write. The better the bookstore and the wider their range, the more effective this exercise is. What you have to do is make the same decisions you would normally make when looking for a book. Your first question upon entering the store is what section is it in? When a title is sold in—as they refer to the process of a bookstore acquiring copies of your book—they have to decide where to shelve it in the shop. That means your book will have to be pigeonholed in one category. As an author, you don't get much of a say on where your book will go—you can tell your publisher, who can recommend that category to the retailers, but that doesn't mean it's where your book will end up. I remember the popular philosopher John Armstrong describing the angst he felt over whether his books should be shelved under philosophy (prestigious, but not huge sales) or self-help (less prestigious, but with the potential to be sold by the box load). In fact, John ended up being the exception to the rule and enjoying the best of both worlds, having his books available to two sets of book buyers. But you don't hear stories like that very often.

So where have they decided to put your book? Is it near the best-sellers or new releases? Is it in a brightly lit, high-traffic area? Or is it in the most coveted position of all—by the coffee machine?! Any one of those is a good result. Of course, there are other spots in the store—down the back, in a dark corner, near the discount section, by the washrooms—but let's hope your book is front and center and in the spotlight. When you've found "your" section, cast your eyes across the shelves. Are the books facing cover out or spine out? If the covers are facing out, that means this is the sort of area where books are moving fast, or at least the retailer wants them to move fast, whereas spine out means not so fast. Retailers use books facing out as a way of creating color and movement to add a bit of excitement and get people reaching into their pockets and wallets at the till. Then have a look at where your book would sit on the shelves. This is where your surname can come in handy if it begins with a letter somewhere in the middle of the alphabet. If, on the other hand, your surname begins with a Z, please don't complain about discriminatory placement on the shelves, as I once heard an author do.

Next, start taking books off the shelves and leafing through them—look for the sort of thing that readers interested in your work might like to read. But be imaginative and think laterally. People rarely stick to a single issue when they buy books. If someone is looking for a title on environmental science, chances are they will also read science in general, books about nature, maybe even a spot of politics. Readers of French history will in all likelihood also be interested in the history of other nations and may well collect books about French art, design, cinema, and food. Once you have collected a handful (an armful if you are bold) of books that your hypothetical reader might be interested in, start by looking at the spines to see the names of the publishers, and note these down. What you are doing here is starting a database of potential publishers to send your publishing proposal to. Then look inside the books and find the acknowledgments sections. After the author has thanked their family, their partner, their faithful dog, and their god, they will thank everyone who has worked on their book at the publishing house. This is very nice for them, but it's pure gold for you. These names are what will change your proposal from an anonymous "Dear Sir/Madam" document to a personalized approach that could well garner interest.

You can do this exercise twice if you like. The second time, go up to the front counter and ask for help. You can either be honest and tell them what you are really doing, or you can pretend to be looking for a book as a present for a friend. And this is where you quickly discover that booksellers are not only an endangered species to be protected at all costs, but they can also be a huge resource and will ultimately become your friends in terms of selling your books. People who work in bookshops do so not because they are looking to get rich quick—because on what they are being paid, they won't— but because they love books. They eat, sleep, and breathe books. And best of all, they know books inside out. If you want to know what sold well, what didn't sell, what people were talking about, just ask a bookseller. So if you tell a bookseller about your idea for a book, they will be able to tell you what else has been written on the subject, how successful those books were, and whether they think your book might sell. And when you do have a published book, they will be delighted to see you in store and to work with you on moving as many units as you can. Just don't do sneaky "author tricks" like rearranging their shelves to make your books look good or signing copies of your book unasked—a signed copy is technically a damaged copy that can't be returned to the publisher if it doesn't sell. If you don't have ready access to a bookstore, especially a good one, you can look in the review pages of newspapers and specialist publications to see what's being reviewed and what's being advertised. It won't give the overall market survey that the shelves of a bookstore will, but it's better than nothing.

PITCHING YOUR BOOK

So you've worked out which publishing houses to pitch to, and you've got a list of names to contact. It's time to take that first step on the journey to being published. Even though this is the first step of many, in some ways, it is probably the most important step, the step you absolutely must get right. The person you pitch your book to has to share your excitement for your project and become your champion. They have to get so excited about your ideas that they are happy to drive them through the often difficult and challenging publishing process. They have to be behind you 100 percent, or this simply won't work. They also have to "get it." They need to understand and share your vision for your book. Your message must be crystal clear right from the start.

At this stage, if you have the platform and profile to convince someone that you are a publishable commodity, it's possible that your book may be no more than just a good idea—you may not even have written it yet. But now it will have to become a full-fledged proposal. A proposal is a demonstration of you as both a clever and imaginative writer and as someone with whom the publisher can have a successful business relationship. The proposal must be creative and strategic, art and craft at the same time. Publishers' websites will tell you what they are looking for, and every one of them does it slightly differently. Some publishers list names and email addresses to pitch to, whereas others just have a general submissions email address. Some publishers will have a day of the week or maybe a week or month every once in a while when they accept proposals— again, their website will tell you this. And while you will need to tailor and individualize every proposal you send in to suit individual publishers' requirements, essentially, they are all looking for a document that looks something like this...

THE RECIPE FOR A CLASSIC PUBLISHING PROPOSAL

Title. This is the very first thing your potential creative and business collaborator will see. What do we know about first impressions? That's right—they count. So come up with the best book title that you can. Of course, it will probably change several times along the route from manuscript to book. Interestingly, the title is often one of the most hotly debated parts of the publishing process, along with the book's cover design.

Then you need to decide if you're going to have a subtitle. They are not compulsory, but they can help explain an obscure title and even give a hint of the style of the book—a subtitle with a sense of humor, for example, hints at a light and very readable book. Make sure the title is set out beautifully—a nice, clean font, lots of white space, and definitely nothing fancy. And do *not*, whatever you do, see this as an opportunity for you to have a go at being a book designer. I cannot emphasize this enough. I have seen far too many well-meaning but truly awful book cover mock-ups. First impressions count, remember?

Contents listing. The beauty of being a nonfiction writer is that you only have to write a couple of chapters of your book before you start selling it to potential publishers—or, if you have a particularly strong reputation and a high profile, you may only need a proposal. But you do need to have a plan for what your finished book will look like, particularly its structure and length. Your publisher is taking a chance on you, hoping that these two brilliant chapters will develop into an equally brilliant book, so they need convincing that you can make that leap. Your contents listing shows them you've mapped out the trajectory of the book.

Summary or rationale. Remember all those books you've picked up and bought simply on the basis of something like "With its searingly drawn characters and tour-de-force storytelling, this gripping drama follows the trials and tribulations of a young researcher battling the evil forces of academia as she races against time—and a dwindling scholarship—to deliver her PhD"? Well, this is your chance to write advertising copy. OK, maybe more substantial than advertising copy, but certainly something that is written in the style of the book itself and shows the sort of content that you propose to deliver. What you are aiming to do is to have the same effect on your editor and publisher as the final version will have on your readers as they browse the shelves of their local bookstore.

Outline. This is where you show the totality of the book. Treat it as a chapter-by-chapter summary, and write it in an intriguing way. Give us the highlights, and show us the tone you will be using to tell your story. If, after reading your outline, the publisher is still unsure of what the book is about and what the reading experience will be like, they probably won't be interested. Remember that you are not only telling the publisher what's in the book—you're also giving them a taste of your writing style.

About the author. Here we are looking for an elegantly drawn portrait that demonstrates your expertise and passion and gives us an idea of your style and readability. If your style is humorous with a lightness of touch, your bio and blurb should match. And if you are a shy wallflower who hesitates to put themselves forward and sees boasting about their own achievements as a little brash and tasteless, then get over it!

Your platform. This can be part of "About the Author" or it can be listed separately, but I hope by now you know what this means. These days, half of the selling of a trade book, and even some scholarly titles, is actually about the author. Your platform is what backs up your salability. Are you known professionally across the country or around the world? Are you the president of your professional association? Do you have a regular newspaper column or radio show? Are you a go-to guest on your local television station's breakfast show? Anything you do that gets you some sort of visibility or even notoriety will do here. And don't worry if that visibility is niche; sometimes a few hundred devoted listeners tuning in to an intelligent fifteen-minute interview on a community radio show will equate to more book sales than hundreds of thousands of listeners for an inane two-minute slot on commercial breakfast radio.

The audience. Who is your reader? As you know by now, there is no generic "general public" who will buy and read anything. There is a series of niche markets determined by subject and writer. So who are your niche markets? Who do you think might buy your book? Be realistic here—speaking at a conference on the witches of Salem doesn't mean your book will be picked up by Harry Potter fans worldwide. In a way, this and the following section are trick questions. The publisher probably instinctively knows who will buy your book. They've been in the business long enough, and they may well have sold similar or related titles, but they are always open to being surprised. If you are aware of potential buyers (and ways of reaching them) that they are not, this is a point in your favor. You both want to sell your books after all.

The competition. This is often referred to as "comp titles," and I have to confess after all these years, I am still confused as to whether *comp* is short for *competing* or *comparable*. I suspect it's probably both. But essentially it is the answer to two questions: What are your readers likely to have already bought and read, and what could they conceivably buy alongside or even in preference to your book? Your publisher will have a good sense of this already, but they are always interested to see your take on this—you will be aware of books they haven't heard of (you are an expert, after all), and they also like to see if you have a commercial sense or a market awareness. Remember how they are seeing you as a business collaborator as well as a provider of creative content? This is where you show them that you mean business. And don't forget "comparable" can come from outside your field; a comparable title can just be an author whose style and approach you aspire to.

Publicity and promotional opportunities. Your publisher will have in-house publicists or freelancers they regularly rely on who will have existing contacts in print and electronic media. They'll probably be able to get you a few radio interviews, maybe a TV slot, and a couple of reviews in the daily or weekend papers. They will have social media covered—certainly in the book and literary fields. But the number of publicists they can call on—freelance or in-house—will be limited by ever-shrinking budgets, and there are likely to be competing demands on your publicist's attention from other book releases. So whatever avenues for marketing and promotion you can come up with will be gratefully received. If you know, for example, that you are giving the keynote at a major conference in your field at the time your book is scheduled to be released and think you can convince the organizers to buy two thousand copies to put in delegates' show bags, tell your publisher, and they will love you for it. If you have a regular column or radio show and can squeeze a mention or two of the book into this, tell them that too. And if the anniversary of the event you are writing about is coming up, let them know about that too. Anything that helps with the sell is good. And of course, you are again demonstrating your commercial-mindedness, something every publisher is looking for in their authors these days.

Sample chapters. This is where the magic happens, and you show the publisher just how good your writing is. Your two chapters can be any two chapters—they don't have to be the first two. It is more important that the writing is as good as you can possibly make it. You only get one shot at this. I've often heard it said that if you are lucky, you might still get a publishing deal with a half-baked proposal and two brilliant chapters, but you'll never get the same response with a stunning proposal and two badly written chapters. It's all about the writing.

Presentation. This is not a section of the proposal but an overall look. Your proposal is a business presentation that is, we hope, going to persuade a commercial publisher to invest tens of thousands of dollars into your book in the hope of making that and a lot more back. Your proposal needs to give them confidence that you are someone worth going into business with. A sloppy-looking, badly written proposal will not do that. A nice, clean, well-laid-out proposal will. At the risk of repeating myself: you often only get one chance at this. Don't get it wrong!

WHAT HAPPENS NEXT?

OK, now that we've put together an impressive proposal, let's get back on the road to publication and look at step two: let's assume the person at the publishing house you contacted with your proposal is interested in your book idea. Maybe they helped you, nurtured you even, to come up with your book proposal, or maybe you did it yourself. Whichever way, you have an impressive document that distills your book into a few pages at most and makes it look publishable.

Your proposal now moves up the line, usually to an acquisitions editor or acquiring publisher. Remember how the message in your proposal has to be absolutely crystal clear, right from the start? This is even more important now that it is out of your hands and others will be representing it on your behalf. If you don't communicate it clearly and concisely to them, what chance do they have of passing on your message?

Now comes step three, where many a young writer has encountered unexpected disappointment: your book proposal goes to the acquisitions meeting, so called because if you pass this hurdle successfully, the publisher will soon acquire the right to publish your work. It's important to note that they are not buying your words. They are acquiring the right to use (or license) your words, in agreed formats, to make money for a specific period of time in a specific geographic territory—money that, all going well, you will share. At this stage, that doesn't really mean anything to you, but in future years—once you have become big and famous and have moved on to another publisher who is interested in adding your early works to their catalogue—it will be quite important.

Yours won't be the only book your acquisitions editor/publisher will take to the acquisitions meeting. And they won't be the only one putting titles forward at that meeting. A large publishing house could easily have ten publishers at the meeting pitching ten books each. That's one hundred book ideas all crying out for attention and one hundred nervous authors with tightly crossed fingers. Unfortunately, no publishing house will have the funds to acquire so many titles at once. The budget will perhaps only stretch to ten or twenty books at most.

Everyone is in the room for this meeting. Sales, marketing, finance, publicity, and design all have input into the decision. They have all read your proposal. If this isn't your first book, they will have used a database called BookScan to check sales figures for any previous books you have written and for the books you are comparing yours to (your comp titles). If you've been published by this house before and rejected all the great ideas your publicist came up with, they will know that too (known in the trade as being "a difficult author"). These meetings can, I am told, be quite brutal. I know one senior publishing figure who refers to the acquisitions meeting as "the bloodbath."

CONTRACTS AND BOOK PRODUCTION

But let's assume your book doesn't fall by the wayside, and your acquiring publisher gets the go-ahead from the meeting to acquire it. You'll get a contract—there may be a few drafts of this until everyone is happy—which is essentially a long legal document, the most important parts of which (as far as you are concerned) are the title, the word count, and the delivery date. Oh, and the money, of course! The money will probably come as a royalty on your sales; this means you will get an agreed percentage on the money taken at the till of your local bookshop on every copy. This could be anything from 5 percent up to 15 percent and may be on the net price or the recommended retail price (you've probably seen the acronym "RRP"). The money may come much later on when the books are actually being sold, or some of it could come in the form of an advance against future sales. The contract will also detail things like territories, translation, film, TV and audio rights, and copyright, all of which you should read and check that you're happy with. If you are uncertain about anything, ask someone else to look at it. And if you are still unsure, you can always buy an hour of a lawyer's time.

The title, as I have said before, will be hotly debated (and it wouldn't hurt to check your contract to see if phrases like *working title* are used so you're not locked into something you hate right from the start), but the word count and the delivery date are what really matter here. The word count determines the physical size of the book (from which things like copyediting, design, printing, and binding can be costed), but it also gives an idea of the type of book we are dealing with; is it a modest, short, easy-to-read book or a sprawling epic spanning two centuries that will challenge your reader with, if nothing else, finding the time to read it? Think of the difference in production costs between Patrick Süskind's 272-page *Perfume* and Gregory David Roberts's *Shantaram,* weighing in at a whopping 944 pages. And the deadline is absolutely crucial. Your publishers will have a carefully planned annual calendar. They will release titles at appropriate times (to coincide with major festivals and events, on a seasonal basis, or even for key selling opportunities like Mother's Day or Father's Day), but they will also spread the titles out so that their probably already overstretched marketing and publicity departments can cope. If you think you won't be able to deliver your completed manuscript on schedule, you'd better tell them as early as possible so they can reschedule. One of the quickest ways to sour a good relationship with a publisher is to call them the night before a deadline to tell them you are "a bit behind." I really cannot emphasize enough how word count and deadline are crucial—in academia, they may have been serving suggestions at best, but in the commercial world, they are the Word of God and not to be trifled with.

It's probably worth throwing in at this point that you might not actually have a book in the physical sense—your title may come out as an ebook. These formats are very much the way of the future and just as valid a publication option as a chunk of dead trees held together by glue. But the rule about deadlines and word counts still stands. Stick to them!

Another option for publishers is print on demand, where books are printed when they are ordered by bookstores and individual readers rather than printed in bulk up front. Some publishers will move a book to print on demand once the initial print run sells out, avoiding any delay in supplying copies if there is an unexpected spike in publicity and awareness—such as when an author wins an award out of the blue or is mentioned in a celebrity blog, or the issue they have written about suddenly resurfaces. Make sure you check with your publisher about their plans if your print run does sell out.

So you sign your contract, you are paid a tiny advance (or not), and you get on with writing your book. Your advance is exactly that—it is an advance against the money you hope you will earn when your book sells. There was a time when every author would get at least some sort of advance for their book. These days, times are much tougher, and it is entirely conceivable that all you might be offered is a contract with no advance. It doesn't mean you won't get paid, of course; it just means you won't see anything until people actually start buying your book.

Then your book is edited, designed, printed, bound together, and turned into a beautiful physical object. Let me tell you, there is nothing as exciting as holding a book with your name on the cover. Thousands of copies of it are packed into boxes, loaded on trucks, and distributed to stores that have taken on your book, both physical and online. At the same time, the book is usually uploaded to various digital platforms so that it can be downloaded and read by readers on their Kindles, iPads, e-readers, phones, and other devices.

DISTRIBUTION AND MARKETING

The traditional book-publishing industry uses a model called "sale or return." When your publisher distributes your book to bookstores, the publisher still owns the books. And for the next three months, while they sit on the bookstores' shelves being picked up, thumbed through, and put down again by hesitant book buyers, the publisher continues to own them. If, at the end of that three-month period, no one has bought your books, they could conceivably be packed back into boxes and sent on a return journey back to the publishers. There are a few exceptions to this rule where books are sold as "firm sale," but generally this is for high-cost, small-print-run books (design, art, architecture, that sort of thing), and when major chain stores bulk-buy large quantities at a high discount.

So all the books you see in your local bookstore, certainly all the new releases, are effectively on loan from the publisher. If they are to survive the three-month initial "loan" period, the book retailer then has to decide to pay for them and keep them on the shelf. Which is why it is entirely possible to take a look at your first royalty statement, see that 3,000 books have gone out of the warehouse, and get very excited, only to be very disappointed six months later by the next statement that shows that 2,999 of them have come back again. It can happen. Let's hope it doesn't, but you need to go in with your eyes wide open.

Next, your book is launched and marketed. When I say "launched," don't expect a big ceremony with speeches and ribbons being cut. Publishers are not fans of expensive book launches these days. Some don't support launches at all, whereas others will offer in-kind support—organizing invitations or securing a bookseller. And, I have to say, I tend to agree with them. By the time your book is being launched, advance copies will have gone out to reviewers, and all the marketing will be in place. A launch is never going to add to that. Of course, if you feel like throwing a party and thanking all your supporters over the long and arduous writing process, go for it! Just don't expect someone else to pay for it.

And now your book sells (or it doesn't sell, but let's be optimistic and hope that it does). Which means you get paid. Or you will get paid...eventually. Publishers tend to do royalty statements (the writer's equivalent of the pay slip) either semiannually or annually. Some multinationals have to send their finances off on a trip to head office in London or New York before they come back, which can add to your waiting time. It can be quite some time before you see even a relatively small amount of money. And remember, if you've had an advance, you may already have been given this money up front. So if you received a $3,000 advance, and your share of book sales in the first six to twelve months is $3,000, your first paycheck will be a big fat zero. Of course, things could be worse—all the unsold books could be returned to the warehouse, and no amount of discounting or special offers will persuade any retailer to take them. If this state of affairs occurs, you will probably be offered the chance to buy your own books at something like a dollar a copy (presumably for you to either give them away or try to sell them yourself) or, failing that, the books will be sent to be pulped. Probably most importantly, however, is that none of this should come as a shock to you, as you will have thoroughly read and understood your contract, won't you? Forewarned is forearmed!

In many ways, book publishing can be an environmentally wasteful and damaging industry, especially if books are simply pulped at the end of it. But print on demand is an alternative, and one that some publishing enterprises have found works for them. When a book is ordered, the publisher will instruct their printer to digitally print one copy of the book (the artwork and copy having been sent beforehand electronically) and mail it off to the buyer, considerably lessening the environmental footprint. Sure, the economics of printing a single copy versus bulk printing a few thousand mean that unit costs are higher, but that price differential is getting smaller and smaller as technology progresses.

• • •

So that's traditional publishing in a nutshell. It's been around for quite a while, and while it is enthusiastically embracing the e-revolution, it is also enjoying the fact that we still seem to like holding a physical book in our hands. But it's still hard work, as any publisher will tell you. However, traditional publishing plus the print-on-demand model and the huge changes in self-publishing we are about to look at mean that you now have a range of options for publication open to you.

24
SELF-PUBLISHING

We live in interesting times: the digital revolution
has thrown the gauntlet down to the world of
publishing, the balance of power is shifting, and
you, as a writer, can now control your own destiny!
OK, you can publish your own work at least.

Like traditional publishing, self-publishing has also been around for a fairly long time, and these days, it's a very exciting and viable option for someone wanting to get their ideas out there and read. Sadly, this hasn't always been the case. Once upon a time, authors paid good money, sometimes quite a lot of it, to a predatory "custom" or "vanity" publishing company for editing, design, printing, distribution—essentially anything the publisher could think up—and at the end of the process received several boxes of badly designed, cheap-looking books. You used to be able to spot a self-published book at one hundred paces—they were that bad.

I'd like to say that this never happens these days, but it does—though less often than it used to. And today's advances in technology mean that the final unsaleable product looks better when sitting on the coffee table (or in boxes in the garage) than it did in the bad old days. But there is a distinct light at the end of the tunnel beckoning us on to a new and exciting version of self-publishing. So let's take a look at how things work now.

The process starts with you being an expert in a particular field. Once you're an expert, you can establish your digital footprint and a degree of visibility in your area of expertise in the ways we've talked about before. This will develop your profile, the first stage in your platform ("Platform 9¾," page 101). Next, you will be noticed by newspaper and magazine editors (possibly with a little help from you, of course) and will then expand into writing short print pieces on your topic—opinion pieces, short background stories, explainers, features, that sort of thing ("Newspapers and Magazines," page 155). If all goes well, you will begin to appear on radio and television ("Working with the Media," page 141) and become the go-to person in your field. All this will feed your public's interest in you until they are no longer simply interested individuals giving you a passing glance but instead a niche market all primed and ready for the words you've been waiting for me to say...a book!

And this is the moment you've been waiting for: you write and self-publish an eagerly awaited book that is snapped up as an ebook or print-on-demand book by the niche market that you have developed and nurtured. How good is that?

It's probably worth spending a moment here on the risk factors associated with the two major forms of publishing. For all its experience and knowledge and insight, traditional publishing is still a risk. Good publishers have amassed huge experience in what does and doesn't sell, and they take great care to select books and authors that they think the market wants to buy and read. But they don't really know. Because if they did, every author would be the next J. K. Rowling or Stephen King. It would be easy to say the risk was all on the part of the publisher—and in a way, it is, certainly in a financial sense—but if you, a writer, sold seventeen copies of your print run of three thousand and are hoping to be signed up for a second book with the same publisher, you're not likely to be in luck. You're in it together, remember?

And self-publishing is not without risk, of course; you are going to have to spend something in the process, and the more you spend, the better your book will look as a general rule, but if you only sell those seventeen copies, you're never going to recoup your investment. I think the trick is building up your potential audience before you publish, possibly even before you put pen to paper. Whether you want to self-publish or work with a traditional publisher, you really can't underestimate the value of creating excitement and anticipation by engaging with potential readers in the lead-up to publication.

Traditionally, once a book had been published, there used to be a prolonged and profound silence. You'd have no idea how many books were being sold, and aside from one or two newspaper reviews, you wouldn't have a clue what people thought of them. As for money, well, that still would be light-years away. These days, you might get coverage on sites like Goodreads or on social media, but you'll still need to go looking for it. Not so in this new version of self-publishing where you've already built up a highly engaged audience who are eagerly awaiting your publication date. As soon as your readers get their hands on your book, you will receive immediate feedback from an audience with whom you've already been in contact for ages. They will put comments on your Twitter feed, post feedback on your blog, or find your address on your website and email you saying how much they love your work. If you have self-published, you will also have a record of every purchaser and will be able to offer them your exciting new book the moment it has been written, assuming you've got them to tick the all-important "I don't mind hearing from you again" box on your site. Of course, any author—both self-published and traditionally published—can engage with their readership through social media or even by responding to online reviews or comments, but the advantage of the self-publishing route is that, if you're doing this right, any interaction is just the continuation of an existing dialogue rather than a response to something that happens after publication. And one big difference is, as a self-published—some might say entrepreneurial—author, you have total control over your brand, and you will receive any money your work makes almost instantaneously. Unheard of in traditional publishing!

ADVANTAGES OF SELF-PUBLISHING

The new version of self-publishing also offers you total freedom, creativity, and control—you really can do anything in your book! And as well as creative freedom, you control your brand and where your book sits under that brand. Unless you're an author with consistent long-term sales potential, a traditional publisher will think of you one book at a time and certainly won't have an eye to your overall brand.

One of the most exciting developments with this new world of publishing is that your book need never be out of date. With traditional publishing, it used to be that it took roughly six months to write a book and another six months to make a book. And then the finished product could easily languish in a warehouse, waiting for its moment to shine for another six to twelve months. I once had a student turned author who, simply because of a chain of unforeseen circumstances, had to wait nearly three years before holding his book in his hand. All of this means that the moment the ink is dry on your book, it is potentially out of date. Certainly, you can't break news or talk about highly topical subjects in this arena. But now your book can be updated with the click of a mouse. If you're selling your own ebook from your website, for example, you just upload the new version to your site and email any existing users to advise them of the update, and if you are selling your book as an ebook for Kindles through Amazon, for example, it will automatically update on your readers' devices.

And if you do decide to go to print, whether it's print on demand or a small run of hard copies for an appearance at a festival, for example, the quality of digital printing these days is pretty much perfect. (Once, it was little better than glorified photocopying and was one of the many reasons that early self-publishing was a fairly tawdry business.)

IS SELF-PUBLISHING RIGHT FOR YOU?

No new development ever comes without challenges, and the new version of self-publishing is no exception. There is still an element of stigma in self-publishing; some believe that books published without the approval of a gatekeeper, i.e., a publisher, might not be of the best quality. There is also a bit of reluctance on the part of mainstream literary media to review or comment on self-published, nonprint, non-traditional format, or electronic works. But if you're not trying to get your book onto the already crowded shelves of your Main Street bookstore, this may be less of a concern. Instead, you may be providing a commodity to an existing market who are aware of it and have already expressed an interest in it.

Some of this goes back to the question of finding the right

publisher for you; in this case, are *you* the right publisher for you? Of course, this is a very personal question that only you can answer. What might be a brave and potentially successful move for one person with an eye to a future as a public figure could be a lethal move for another person aiming for a long-term career in academia.

COSTS

With this new version of self-publishing, it is perfectly possible to go all the way from an idea to an ebook without spending a single cent. There is so much freeware out there that every stage of the process can be accomplished to a reasonably high standard without any expenditure at all. But in life, you really do get what you pay for, so there are areas where, if you want to come across as a total professional and produce a "quality book," you might want to reach into your pocket.

You will almost certainly be going to distribute your book from your own website, so you could spend a little on hosting and web design so that the first port of call for your customers looks as good as it can. This might mean choosing a memorable name for your site, acquiring that name, and then paying a service to host it, then linking it to a professional-looking mail service so that you can email people from yourname@yourwebsite.com. None of these are massive costs, and assuming you start to earn income from your writing, they should be tax-deductible expenses for your business operation. As always, talk to your accountant about that.

If you are selling off your website, you can also look into an ecommerce package. Again, the cheap and cheerful approach is perfectly acceptable—especially when you are starting out—but we hope there will come a time in your professional growth and development when you are moving so many units (to borrow a phrase from physical publishing) that you'll need to replace an email and a PayPal payment with a shopping cart arrangement.

I've mentioned an accountant a few times now—you might already be using one to maximize your annual tax return, but if you're not and you're now venturing into writing for profit, accounting and even legal services are other areas where splashing a bit of cash will help with the professionalism of your operation.

Then we get to the writing and the book itself. Editing can make a huge difference, and there are many, many highly professional freelance editors out there who would be more than happy to make your words shine. And design, layout, and typesetting (especially cover design) will have a significant impact on the look of the book. Many of these services can be found online at quite affordable rates. Search, do your research, compare, and negotiate, and a relatively small outlay could have quite a significant return.

Obviously if you're printing and mailing a print-on-demand title, you will need to factor in the costs of mailing bags and postage, but I'm assuming if you're at this advanced stage, you will have done a fully costed budget for getting your book from author to consumer. And if you are spending anything at all on getting your book published, you should have worked out the breakeven point—the number of sales required to take your book from expensive hobby to profitable enterprise.

Marketing and publicity are two more areas where professionals really can make a difference. The good news is that there are plenty of lean and hungry marketing and publicity people out there who love the sort of challenge a book by someone like you represents. We've talked about how working with the media is based on relationships;

professional marketers and publicists already have these contacts and relationships in place. They can quickly generate the sort of aware- ness and interest in your book that would take you ten times longer and a lot of luck to achieve.

• • •

Let's finish our look at the new world of self-publishing with a thought about the future: your future. At the moment, an ebook is a print book that hasn't been printed. The ideas contained in it might be amazing, but in a technological sense, it really isn't anything special. But you can challenge and, I am guessing—hoping, even— change this. I am looking forward to seeing what the next generation of great minds will do when they decide to turn their attention to the publishing industry. We really do live in interesting times!

25

BUT WAIT, THERE'S MORE!

Where else can you tell the world about your research? Time to look at the other exciting options available to you, such as exhibitions, documentaries, podcasts, and even those theme park rides and arena spectaculars I mentioned before.

The written word and the spoken word, in all their glorious incarnations, are great ways to tell people about your work. But there are other exciting ways to spread the word, many of which are yet to be conceived. They will be thought up by the next generation, and the one after that, using technology that isn't even at beta testing stage yet.

But whatever the next step of the communication revolution turns out to be, what is more important is how we make use of it. What will your answer be when someone asks you to talk about your research in a yet-to-be-invented way? You'll say yes, won't you? Of course you will! In fact, I seriously think, unless what is being proposed is somehow morally or ethically unpalatable, the answer should always be yes.

But for now, let's look at some of the alternatives to print, screen, and public presentations. Here are three ways of getting the word out that I think are worth looking at in more detail—podcasts, exhibitions, and documentaries.

26
PODCASTS

Media has now become very much an on-demand thing, and audio content is no exception. Podcasts are another highly accessible and exciting arena where you can talk about your research.

Podcasts are big. Like the radio programs of old, crossbred with audiobooks and sprinkled with a little digital production magic, they can be everything from very simple exercises in storytelling to big production numbers with a cast of thousands. And they are a form that, without too much investment in time, money, resourcing, and technology, you can master.

As usual, we start with finding the right stories within our research to share. To do this, we must, of course, put ourselves into the minds (and ears) of our audience. Who do we want to communicate our research to? Who are we doing this for? Then, with a picture of the audience in our heads, we ask ourselves what these people might be interested in. Really, if done well, pretty much any topic can form the basis of an interesting podcast.

Ask a dozen friends what podcasts they are listening to, and you'll likely receive at least a dozen different answers—anything from food, science, and culture in *Gastropod* to epidemics and medical mysteries in *This Podcast Will Kill You* to an academically accurate and highly entertaining look at American history in *BackStory*. There are a lot of true crime podcasts—*Casefile* is a particularly good example—and I personally love *Everything Is Alive*, where everyday objects come alive and tell you their stories. And a year doesn't seem to go by without Irish-Australian writer and historian Siobhán McHugh winning an award for one of her excellent podcasts.

There are essentially seven basic types of podcast:

- **Solo commentary:** You, a microphone, and a laptop. That's pretty much it. Of course, you still need to come up with scintillating content, but you can do it all on your own.
- **The one-on-one interview:** As above, plus a guest.
- **A panel show:** Featuring more than one guest being interviewed or a group of guests in discussion.
- **Nonfiction narrative storytelling:** Here you can bring episodes from the past to life or dramatize parts of your research process. A bit more production needed here.
- **Fictional storytelling:** Anything goes with this format.
- **Hybrid:** A nice mix and match of all of the above. A podcast like this can function in the same way that a magazine does.
- **Repurposed/preexisting content:** The audio version of archival footage. There is so much content out there in archives just waiting to be brought out and given a new life. Why not use it?

The world of podcasts is already a fairly well-supplied market, so it's important to stand out. In that case, what makes a good podcast?

The first and most obvious answer would have to be expertise. Far too many podcasts come out of the mouths of well-meaning but ill-informed amateurs. This is your first point of difference. And of course, as with all forms of communication, knowing and understanding your audience will also put you ahead of the pack in this very competitive world.

PODCASTING TIPS

Almost as important as knowing your audience is **knowing your guests**. This will ensure you get the best out of them. I'm all for a bit of spontaneity, but a podcast that is going to be out there forever is not the place to be fumbling in the dark.

Getting the length right is also crucial. While there is no right or wrong answer to this, there are definitely lengths of show that fail to satisfy and other lengths where the show palpably overstays its welcome. I have seen research that puts seventeen minutes as the perfect length for a podcast. As a general rule, I'd suggest you aim for shorter rather than longer, and hey, why not even try seventeen minutes if that feels right?!

Enthusiasm and energy will take you a long way when getting ready to enter the world of podcasting, but at some point, **serious planning, rehearsal, and practice** will need to come into play. This is not that far removed from staging a performance, and with the sole exception of improvisation, you wouldn't do that without having a damned good idea of what's coming next, would you?

I also think **releasing your episodes at regular intervals** that you advertise ahead of time is another good way of establishing and building a loyal listenership. Again, it's all about planning and scheduling.

We are creatures of habit and quite like a spot of familiarity. Podcast audiences are no exception to that rule, so a good series of podcasts will aim for **consistency of style and structure**. You should try to aim for consistency in these areas:

- **Format:** Think of your podcast as a magazine; most successful magazines might vary their content, but their contents page will often look very similar from week to week.
- **Style, tone, and feel:** Just as changing from serious to funny halfway through a book or article will jar your reader, so changing the style or tone or the feel of the show across a series of podcasts will make for a less than satisfactory listening experience. The segments within your shows can be enormously varied; they just need to sit within a known format.

Unless you make it a feature of your podcasts that each and every one features a different "guest" host, your audience will be listening for the familiar, reassuring voice of a **regular host**. All your on-air talent is important, but none is as crucial to the success of the program as the host. A good host understands their audience and sees the program as a conversation with them. They know their subject matter well (and if they don't, they find out about it) and prepare for every interview. Because this is a recording of a live "performance," they warm up and they always rehearse—even the spontaneous bits. A good host knows how to use a microphone well and will set the guests at ease.

You can create a very familiar feel through the use of the same **music, intro and outro sequences, and bumpers** (more on these below). They should become as familiar to your audience as the masthead of their favorite newspaper.

TECHNOLOGY

Now, while anyone can produce a podcast for very little money, you probably should think about spending a small amount of funds to make sure you get the tech right. You will need good **microphones** to record with and good **headphones** to monitor what you are recording and listen back to it. You really should use over-the-ear headphones, not earbuds, to make sure you are only hearing what you are recording, and stay well away from noise-cancelling technology as it just paints a completely false picture of what your listeners will eventually hear. And unless you pay a small fortune, headphone-microphone sets are usually substandard.

Interestingly, while our eyes are very forgiving when it comes to wobbly, low-resolution camera shots and homemade graphics, our ears are extremely unforgiving. All it takes is the tiniest bit of background noise for us to throw our arms up, exclaim "Amateur hour!" and tune out. So make sure you **sound good**.

You'll need a **pop filter** to stop a weird sound from happening every time you use the letters b or p—they don't cost much—and **stands** for your microphones, ideally with built-in suspension, so that when your guest leans forward to make a particularly eye-opening revelation, you don't hear the creaking of the desk as much as you hear the salacious details.

And you'll need to download and install some **audio recording and editing software**. You shouldn't need to pay for any of this; there is plenty of very good freeware out there. You'll also need what is called **ID3 tagging software**—another easy-to-use piece of software that will add all the metadata you need to your podcast. Googleability again, folks.

You should bring your podcast to life by using **music and sound**

effects (again, this shouldn't cost you a penny, as there is heaps of perfectly good royalty-free content out there), and **postproduction and editing** will make sure your podcast is as good as it can possibly be. Remember how crowded and competitive the world of podcasts is? You need to do anything you can to stand out.

Make sure you **edit yourself.** Really edit yourself heavily: edit your script or notes beforehand, then edit what you record afterward. And be a little theatrical. Hell, be a lot theatrical if you want! Your podcast is your stage, and you can be a performer. A good podcast is not hastily thrown together but is well planned, scripted, and edited.

If you do all that and do it well, you will have yourself a half-decent podcast.

YOUR PODCAST IN ACTION

Now, let's try an exercise to look at the elements of a podcast that really bring it to life and make it more professional: the intro ("Welcome to..."), the outro ("You have been listening to..."), and the bumpers—those little stings that are played in between segments to bridge the gap ("You are listening to...").

Have a go at scripting the opening and closing of your show and the bumpers. Your intros and outros should be roughly thirty seconds or about seventy-five words long and should tell your audience

- **the name of your podcast** (usual rules for a title apply—catchy, witty, memorable, right?);
- **where it comes from** (as global as the online world is, we still like to hear that you are broadcasting from the basement of a haunted bookstore in Prague);

- **the purpose or tagline** of the podcast (are you shining a light on rocket science or bringing to life stories from Tudor times, for example?);
- **the episode title and number**, if you are numbering them; and
- **any other important data** (the name of your network, the recording date if that's relevant, sponsors if you are lucky enough to have any, or disclaimers you feel you should make).

While you are doing this, think about the sort of music and sound effects you might use. Ideally, you'll use the same music and sound effects in every episode to give your regular listeners something they can become used to.

Your bumper is typically a fifteen-second segment that is dropped in to introduce a new segment of the episode or to create smooth transitions between different segments. In a way, it's the glue that holds the program together. It often stylistically reflects the intro and outro and might use a truncated version of your "theme music," for example.

Once you've come up with an idea for your intros, outros, and bumpers, just to take the exercise a little further, lean into an imaginary microphone, pretend you are the host, and introduce yourself—give your name and a little mini biography, if you like. Then introduce what the show is going to be about or summarize the episode, and tell your audience who your guests are going to be for this show.

If you can do all this, you're well on the way to successful podcasting.

• • •

Of course, as with all new media, producing a good product is only half the story. How will you get people to listen to your podcasts?

While they will be physically hosted elsewhere, you can embed them into your website or your social media or use that social media to advertise their existence. If you mount the right campaign in advance, they can turn into a hotly anticipated commodity rather than a surprise to your friends, followers, and fans.

27

EXHIBITIONS

Take your research off the page or screen and
put it up on the wall or mount it on a plinth, then
stand back and watch the crowds pour in.

E xhibitions are a great way to take your work to the next level.
Not only do they give you the opportunity to come up with
creative and exciting ways of presenting your ideas, but the
numbers of people who visit exhibitions can be staggering. Sure,
we're not all at the level of the terra-cotta warriors or Leonardo's
inventions, but to take part in an exhibition in your average city or
regional museum could potentially see your work shown off to tens
of thousands of people—or more.

So to ease you into this more visual way of thinking about your
work, let's start by getting your imagination going. This is an exercise I use quite a lot, and it's amazing how effective it is in getting
researchers and academics to think like museum professionals.

Close your eyes, and imagine a white room. White walls, white
ceiling, white floor. This is the blank canvas on which you are going
to start painting a visual representation of your ideas.

You see four plinths—again, these are painted white. You can decide how big they are and where they sit in the room. On each of these plinths, I want you to place an object that conjures up some aspect of your research. Because this is an imaginative exercise, don't let physical constraints or budget restrict you. Defy the laws of physics if you want to.

OK—all four objects in place? Now let's get interpretive. Each of these plinths needs a label—up to fifty words each—that expands on what the spectator is looking at. Remember, you don't need to tell us what we can see; you need to help us understand it. Tell the story of the object—its background and its history, with some human interest.

Now we get to go high tech. On one of your walls—again, you can choose which one and how big—you are going to project a silent sixty-second video loop. This video loop can be as abstract or as realistic as you want, but again it must trigger aspects of your research in the mind of your audience.

Lastly, we are going to play with sound. Imperceptibly built into the room's walls is a high-end surround-sound system. (I told you budget was no problem.) I want you to come up with a five-minute sound loop that visitors to your room will hear. As with all the elements we've added so far, it is contributing to the overall picture and creating a mood, an atmosphere that helps your audience understand your work.

Now stand back and look at—and listen to—what you've got. You've just put together the first draft for the design of a room in a very stylish exhibition devoted to your work and the ideas it raises.

I have seen some really imaginative responses to this exercise: bushfire researchers who have produced very visceral experiences using the sights, sounds, and even smell of fire; climate change investigators who have brought the plight of drought-affected farmers home to the audience through simple yet gut-wrenching videoed interviews; and neuroscientists who used a giant, high-tech model of the human brain to show how the human mind works.

And as an afterthought, if you want to give your exhibition a title, maybe even think up a look for the poster and program, please go ahead—it's your exhibition, after all!

CREATING AN EXHIBITION

Being involved in the creation of an exhibition is very exciting, but it's also hugely different from the very solitary role of writer or researcher. To begin with, you are obviously no longer working alone; you are part of a team of amazing people. And your role will change—in an exhibition team, you could be a researcher, writer, or story consultant. How you tell your research story is also going to change dramatically if you get to work on an exhibition. Suddenly you are in the world of nonlinear, nonnarrative stories. Forget any beginning, middle, and end approaches you might have used in the past. Exhibitions provide glimpses, tastes, and suggestions that can be consumed in any order yet still tell a cohesive story.

If you are thinking of moving into exhibitions, you need to ask yourself a couple of key questions up front: What's the one, big, overarching idea (the glue, if you like) that holds your exhibition together? Who are you doing it for? This isn't too far removed from thinking about your writing when you are trying to get it published. You also need to get to know your potential client—the museum or gallery that you think might want to stage your show. Look at their website and past programs. What sort of exhibitions do they stage?

Who seems to be their audience? Are they "right" for you? You'd be wasting your time to propose a small local exhibition (a history of your suburb, for example) to a museum whose recent offerings are shows like *The Masterpieces from the Hermitage*, *Walking with Dinosaurs*, and *Queens of Egypt*.

You also might like to think of your work as part of a bigger story. Your research might be narrow and focused on one aspect of the human body (eyesight, for example), but a group of researchers all tackling different but related specializations could put together a fascinating look at the human body through the prism of the five senses.

PITCHING YOUR IDEA

And then, as with your writing, to turn your idea into reality, you need to put together a proposal. It is very much like a publishing proposal ("Traditional Publishing," page 188)—a sales pitch document that aims to catch the eye and imagination of someone who might want to work with you, so it needs to be both imaginative and businesslike. A typical exhibition proposal would set out

- **an idea for a title** that will get people to put their hands into their pockets and buy tickets;
- **the big idea**, expressed as clearly and in as few words as possible;
- **the content you want to include**, to give an idea of what might need to be assembled and the technical requirements, such as wall space, plinths, display units, audiovisual equipment;
- **how the content will be interpreted** (remember that the audience needs to understand your content);
- **the look or feel or atmosphere of the exhibition** (will it be fairly neutral or fully immersive, for example?);

- **the audience** (who is the exhibition for, and what sort of visitor experience are they going to have?); and
- **who you are** and what you think your role in the team could be, showing that you know your stuff *and* you also "get" how an exhibition might be put together.

Your proposal document needs to be part of a bigger campaign. You should have done a fair bit of homework about the institution you want to work with. You should have visited it and know your way around it. And you should have some idea in your head of how your proposed exhibition could fit into their physical space, their style of programming, and their schedule of shows. Then you'll make contact with someone and have a cup of coffee and a chat. All going well, at this point, they will say to you, "Why don't you send me something?" Which is where your proposal comes into play. Making contact beforehand and soliciting an informal invitation to pitch will always receive a much more positive response than cold-calling with a proposal.

Exhibitions are hard work, but if you thought holding a book with your name on it was exciting, wait until you have a framed poster on the wall and can wear the T-shirt and dry your dishes with the souvenir tea towel of your research!

28
DOCUMENTARIES

Swap your paper and pen or laptop for a
camera and microphone, and bring your
research to life in a whole new way.

Another "out there" way of communicating your research
that is worth exploring in more detail is documentaries.
The term *documentary* is a very general label that covers
anything onscreen that is nonfiction—this can mean investigative
reports, issue-based films, how-to films, audiovisual content for use
in exhibitions, advocacy films, exposés, and biographies. And documentaries can be everything from cheap and cheerful productions
shot on a phone and edited on a laptop all the way up to big-budget,
high-tech spectaculars requiring large crews and tons of equipment,
coming soon to an IMAX screen near you.

Why don't we try another imaginative exercise to get you thinking about the possibilities of documentary in the same way we introduced exhibitions?

Start by thinking of a single object that symbolizes, sums up, or
somehow represents your research or one facet of your research.

Then imagine how you would show it on camera—is it a flat two-dimensional object that simply fills the screen, or is it framed by the camera somehow? Or is it a three-dimensional object that can't be seen from a single angle? In this case, how would you use the camera to show it to your audience? Would you be up close and personal with a close-up or detached and distant with a long shot? Would you have the power and authority of a static shot or the livelier, more dynamic look of a moving shot with your camera panning, tilting, or zooming?

Now that you have your opening shot—sometimes called your "establishing shot"—think of a piece of music and a series of sound effects that add a layer of meaning to your object. How would they be heard? Are they in the foreground or far off in the background? Describe them in as much detail as you can, and remember not only to describe the content but also how that content sounds. If it's dialogue, for example, whose voices are we hearing? Is the voice whispered into the microphone, or is it a distant cry?

And finally, write the first line or two of a narrative that goes with the object and the music and sound effects you have just chosen. Again, it's not just about the words. What will those words sound like? What sort of person would do the voiceover? How would they sound?

There you go! In a few short seconds, you've come up with the opening of a documentary that brings your research to life in a whole new way. Again, go crazy and give it a title if you like.

GETTING STARTED

Documentaries are a lot like exhibitions: both have to be very well organized and executed, with the route from A to B carefully calculated and planned and definitely not treated as a voyage of discovery. Ask yourself why you want to make a documentary. Is documentary the best way to communicate this aspect of your work? Do you have a particularly visual message you want to get across? Is your subject just crying out to be filmed?

One of your early but very important decisions will be where and how your documentary will be seen. Will it be seen as a standalone element on a screen in its own right? And will that be the big screen, as in free-to-air TV or streaming service or satellite or cable, or will it be the small screen—an in-flight video, say, or YouTube? Or is it part of something else, like an exhibition, your website or blog, or an online project?

Documentaries cost money; you will need funding. This might come from formal sources, like government grants and philanthropic trusts, or from organizations related to your field of research that offer grants for projects in the field. Think as broadly as possible about sources of funds—even social media can be a source of money these days if you decide to conduct a crowdfunding campaign. And you could always hold a fundraising event, if you thought that might work—everyone likes a party, right?

You will also probably need some sort of pitch document or prospectus to leave with potential supporters. This should detail the following things:

- **The title:** As always, your title should capture the imagination and tell us something but not necessarily everything about your story.
- **What it is about:** Keep this short, sharp, and to the point. A reader shouldn't be left in any doubt as to what your film will

look, sound, and feel like and how it will hook your audience in and keep them watching through to the end.

- **Length, format, key personnel, and locations:** These practical things should be included.

- **Why you are the best person to make this documentary:** Sell yourself a little here.

- **Who the audience is:** Backers will want to know who and where the audience for your documentary is. Will your idea attract local, nationwide, or even global interest?

- **Where the film will be seen:** If someone is investing as a sponsor, they will want to know where your film will be seen.

So how do you bring your project into being?

PREPRODUCTION

First, there's **research**. Preproduction starts with two phases of research—first the sort of pure research you have spent your whole life doing whereby you assemble facts, figures, stories, and anecdotes, and then field research, which is a more practical, often on-location look at the elements you might be assembling to make your film. Both of these phases happen before you write your script.

Field research—which includes scouting out locations and deciding where to film particular scenes—is particularly important for the scriptwriting process. You can't describe what you haven't seen and use it as an illustration of your story or visual evidence for your argument unless you know it exists and have seen it for yourself.

Next, there's the **script**. Once all your research is in place, then you move on to the script. As a scriptwriter, you have to think in pictures; you have to learn to see like a camera. It's a bit of a cliché, but when you see film directors holding their hands up to make a frame to look through, that's essentially what they are doing. Then, in the script, you need to describe what you want the viewer to see in terms of concrete images, even if you are dealing with more abstract ideas. Quite simply, to be recorded onscreen, things have to be solid and tangible.

You might have seen narrative film scripts before that are almost all dialogue with a few stage directions thrown in. But a documentary script is almost all description. It's best to use simple language such as concrete nouns and strong verbs, and don't be tempted to dress up your prose with adverbs and adjectives.

The typical components you will probably use to tell your documentary story and include in your script are as follows:

- **Interviews:** These may be archival interviews or new ones.
- **Background and establishing shots:** These are often of natural or constructed landscapes and environments.
- **Objects:** These can really fire up the imagination of your audience. You can show them as still images or pan around them or zoom in or out to bring them to life.
- **Archival footage:** This brings authenticity and adds to the production values of the film. Archival footage doesn't have to be historical but may be recently recorded material.
- **Reconstructions:** These can be highly effective in some circumstances, but they do require a lot more resources and inject an element of fiction into a nonfiction project. You may need actors, props, costumes, sets, makeup, special effects, exotic locations, permit fees, licenses, insurance, and police permission, all of which can be very costly and time-consuming to organize.

- **Graphics:** Animations, schematics, diagrams, captions, or charts can form part of your toolkit.

- **Narration:** Whether your narrator is offscreen or onscreen, this is a very simple yet surprisingly effective way to advance your narrative, convey information, or convince us of your argument, but use it sparingly. If we can see something with our eyes, we don't need a voice-over to tell us what we are seeing.

PRODUCTION: TECHNICAL ASPECTS

Any shot, no matter how gripping or interesting it might be, can get boring after a while. **Cutaways** are a great way to prevent this from happening. They can be anything you like; they are simply a shot where the camera cuts away to something else, hence the name. Look at a classic vox pop interview on the news—even something as short as that will be peppered with reaction shots of the interviewer, close-ups of the interviewee's hands fiddling nervously, a wide shot of the landscape, or even a close-up of a street sign reminding the viewer of the location of the interview.

Make sure to use a **variety of different shots and angles** and vary between static shots and moving shots. As with writing and speaking, anything that is the same for an extended period of time gets boring.

Think about the different effects you achieve with **smooth editing versus "jump cuts."** There was a time when jump cuts were to be avoided at all costs; they used to be seen as quite jarring and even confronting. Now they are quite acceptable as ways of joining shots together, especially since the advent of rock video clips and on into the YouTube era. Certainly, if you want a detached and analytical viewer who does not succumb to the suspension of disbelief, a jump cut will do the trick. Brechtian alienation, anyone?

Never hesitate to do **more than one take**, even if you are doing something fairly spontaneous like interviewing people. Your subjects will be perfectly understanding if an airplane roars into shot and drowns out their answer halfway through the take. There's absolutely nothing wrong with restaging key moments to make sure they achieve maximum impact.

Don't trust your ears and eyes. They will often tell you what they think you want to know rather than what's actually happening out there. Your ears will smooth out extraneous noises like distant cars or helicopters, and your eyes won't notice the kid in the corner of the shot picking his nose because they are concentrating on the interviewee in the center of the frame. Always listen through your headphones and look through the viewfinder or monitor. You'll hear and see so much more. And make sure you always review your shots after you've called out "Cut!"

And you are allowed to channel your inner Quentin Tarantino or Steven Spielberg and direct "the talent." Talent, by the way, is a film and TV term that is used quite widely these days. It simply indicates the person in question's position—you are either in front of the camera and are "talent" or behind the lens and are "crew." It has nothing to do with any innate ability, skill, or...talent!

PRODUCTION: INTERVIEWING

Interviews allow you to introduce real-live characters into your story and bring it to life, but you might be a little shocked to discover how unspontaneous the interviews in documentaries really are. You start by preinterviewing—you have a chat with your interviewees, doing a fairly informal version of what you think you might end up with as the formal interview, but also talking about the topic in general. While this doesn't necessarily have to be recorded in any way, you definitely want to make notes.

Then you prepare your questions and write out a script for the interviews, including what you expect the interviewees to say. That's right—anticipate their answers based on your initial discussion. Then, when you do conduct the interviews, ask questions that will result in the sorts of answers you are looking for. While there are documentaries that do include spontaneous, unscripted, and unrehearsed interviews, programs that convey research-based information do not. A decision you will have to make at some point is whether you want your questions to be heard in the soundtrack or not. There is no right or wrong answer, but most audiences are smart enough to work out what the original question was if they hear your interviewees' answers.

Once you've done your final interviews, a transcript of the parts you want to use will form part of your final script.

POSTPRODUCTION

Once your filming is out of the way, you then move into postproduction.

Although film editing is now something you can do yourself—all you need is a laptop and some editing software—it can be a time-consuming process and can often involve getting a specialist editor in. To make it as smooth and painless as possible, you should do what's called a "paper edit"—a description, as accurate as possible, of what you aim to do with the technology when you do the real edit.

You can describe when you want to cut ("when the tall boy in the red hoodie walks out of shot") or use the timing encoded into your footage. If you do a good job, you should be able to read the paper edit and know what you are going to see onscreen in the final cut. You definitely don't want to waste your time (let alone your editor's time) while you search for a story in the footage you have acquired.

Then you edit. Or, if you aren't confident doing this, you beg, persuade, or pay someone else to edit for you. Editing onscreen has strong connections to editing on the page, or at least it involves a similar mindset. People who are good at editing tend to be very objective and analytical and won't be fazed by the idea of going over and over a particular cut, shaving it by a fraction of a second at a time until it looks just right. The rest of us tend to go mad doing this.

• • •

Making documentaries can be a little bit addictive; you rarely meet someone who's made "just the one." The trials and tribulations you can go through to get your work on the screen can be grueling, but when you do see your research burst into life in glorious color and crisp, clear sound, you may find it hard to go back to words on the page again.

And...cut!

6

THE BIZ

29

SHOW ME THE MONEY!

You're in business now—time to look like you
mean business. Here's how to manage your parallel
career as a writer, communicator, and expert.

W e're going full circle now and coming back to your
newfound second career as a professional writer and
communicator. Here's a good exercise to get you in the
right mindset. Imagine that sometime this year, you're going to be
on a panel at your local writers' festival. Festivals are big these days—
there are more and more of them every day, not just in the major
cities but spread throughout the regions as well. And their interest no longer lies exclusively in books. You are just as likely to see
a filmmaker or a scientist or podcaster on the program as you are a
mainstream writer. Which is good for you. So think about the sort of
festival you are appearing in. Where do they hold it? What's it like?
How many people attend? And if you don't know the answers to
those questions, you might want to think about finding out. Writers'
festivals are great places to meet people, to be seen, and, importantly,
to sell your wares.

Once you have a picture of the festival in your head, tell me: What is the panel you are going to appear on called? What is it about? Who else is on it (and here you can be as hypothetical as you like and pick the biggest names to sit next to you)? And when the host or facilitator leans into the microphone to tell the audience about the people they will be spending the next hour or so listening to, how will you be introduced?

That was a bit of fun, wasn't it? Now do the same exercise, but fast-forward ten years. Answer the same questions, but come up with answers that take into account ten years' worth of hypothetical fame, success, and fortune. Especially that introduction to the audience at the end.

That was still fun, right? But this time, there was a little more serious intent involved. You see, with simple exercises like this, you can actually determine where you want to be in ten years' time. Now, if you want to go ahead and do a twenty-year version, be my guest, but this time, try it with a little more strategic thought, perhaps with a plan and timelines.

So what do you have to do when you extend your academic work into professional writing and communicating (other than to write and speak, of course) to achieve those goals?

SETTING UP AS A BUSINESS

To begin with, you need to decide how you are going to trade. You are going to be providing a service to a client, and they are—we hope—going to pay you for this. So you need to become a sole proprietor with a business registration, or a small business, or whatever the appropriate legal setup is where you live. Usually the regulations governing this are fairly easy to understand and follow. You will be very pleasantly surprised, I think, when you see the sorts of resources that are available online to help you with this. If you Google "small business" and your state, not only will you find government resources but also the local chapters of organizations set up to help people just like you.

When you're starting out, aim for the simplest legal and financial structure you can find. Your initial earnings will be relatively small, and I doubt you're looking to do lots of exciting accounting-based paperwork, are you? Later on, you can revisit this. I've seen all sorts of structures used by successful writers—family trusts, limited companies, and the like, all designed to maximize the income and minimize the tax, I would imagine. Remember Idan Ben-Barak and his microbes? Idan went on to become very successful, and his first book was translated into many languages over the years. Every time a new language edition came out, he'd pop into the office and give me a copy. When he was on to something like his sixth translation, I said to him, "You understand the beauty of all this, don't you? Whenever you're on holidays in one of these places, just pop into a bookstore, sign a couple of books, and call your trip a promotional visit. Think of what that could do for your taxes!" He looked at me with a wry smile and replied, "Yes. And if only I earned enough from my books to pay taxes, that'd be great." This from a successful writer. So— simple to begin with, right?

Unless you've had the time and inclination to do a financial management course, I think you'd be best finding yourself an accountant if you start to earn real money for your work outside the university. Some things are best left to experts.

Ensure you keep good records; your accountant will thank you for it, the IRS will thank you for it, and in the long run, you'll realize how much time, effort, and money you have saved yourself. I know many a disorganized artist who's finally decided to come clean with the IRS and arrived at an accountant's office with several shoeboxes full of receipts, only to be amazed that they are going to be charged for the accountant's time to sort out the mess.

MAKING CONNECTIONS

To begin with, you need to get the latest writers' directories for the countries you'd like to target with your writing. These are often referred to as the "bibles" of the industry, and they tell you how to contact each publication, the process for submission, and whether they will pay you. Sitting on my desk is a well-thumbed copy of *The Australian Writer's Marketplace*, which these days is an online publication. In the States, you need look no further than LiteraryMarketPlace.com, while a writing teacher friend of mine tells me his students often refer to Submittable and Duotrope.

You should really think about setting up a "proper" email address—something that demonstrates your professionalism as a writer. Gmail is OK. A university address is good. Your own domain name is best. But hellokittybigboyhotstuff4378561@hotmail.com isn't. It really isn't.

Next you need to establish a social media presence. You know this. We've talked about it before in "Your Googleability." You need to be googleable.

You will need some sort of database. We're not talking anything sophisticated here, certainly not at first. A simple spreadsheet will do. All you want to do is to be able to record and recall who you pitched stories to, whether those pitches were successful, and whether you've been paid. If you ever get to the stage where that level of detail is too hard to deal with, you'll probably be so successful that you'll need to engage a business manager or agent.

In terms of paperwork, you only need to learn how to produce one document—an invoice. (There's a sample one at the end of this book.) It's the simplest thing in the world, and it means you will be paid. A quick look around the internet will give you plenty of examples to look at, but all it needs is

- your name, address, and contact details;
- your business registration number (depending on how your business is set up);
- who you are invoicing and their contact details;
- exactly what you are billing them for;
- how much you are billing them for; and
- where you want the money to end up.

If you get it wrong or your client needs additional information, they will let you know soon enough. The template for an invoice on page 247 is easy to adapt; feel free to put in your details and use it as your own.

STEPPING OUT INTO THE WORLD

To make it at all in your wider engagement—whether writing, speaking, or transforming into a go-to expert—you will need to develop a thick skin and an optimistic outlook. You will be rejected, knocked back, or just plain ignored again and again and again. But it is rarely personal. It's rarely to do with you. Someone will beat you to the pitch, the newspaper or magazine you're trying to get into will change direction, or something major will happen and the front page will get wiped clean. It happens. More often than you'd think. But then suddenly one day, you won't be ignored, and someone will ask to see your story or invite you to speak. But you must understand that you are in it for the long haul.

You will need to think strategically as well as creatively. There are two halves to your life as a writer or speaker. There's the creative side that comes up with great ideas and gets them on the page, all neat and tidy and beautifully written, or in front of an audience complete with dazzling slides and witty repartee. But then there's the strategic, business side of your life. This side of you works all the connections to get your stories in print or the personal appearances booked and then does everything you can to maximize your exposure and lay the groundwork for the next piece you intend to pitch or public event you are to star at.

So how do you get work? Let me tell you "The Story of the Writer." In many ways, this is the story of an archetypical writer, but in fact, this is a real live writer I met years ago when presenting to a room full of emerging writers. I had been invited as the director of the local writers' festival; the director of the local writers' center sat next to me, and this man was "the writer" on the panel. What I find interesting is that, to this day, I can't for the life of me remember his name, but his story has stuck in my head.

So this is how he would work. He'd contact the local newspaper—he'd do it by phone or fax (remember them?) and offer them a story. "Hi there. I've got five hundred words on Paris," he'd say as an opener. "Really? Well, Paris has been done to death so we're not—" But before they could say no, he'd cut them off. "OK. Well, I've also got five hundred words on Berlin." Or maybe they'd say five hundred words was too short, in which case he'd have a thousand words up his sleeve. Or five hundred could have been too long, in which case he'd whip out a two-hundred-word article. In fact, his first and most important skill was never taking no for an answer. He could dance on his toes and think at lightning speed to the extent that, while they might reject his first idea and then his second idea and even his third idea, at some point, he'd wear them down, and they'd give in with a sigh and say, "OK, let's have a look." And this is when he'd start researching and writing. Not a moment before.

Which brings us to his second skill. Fast, furious, accurate, and elegant writing. He'd throw together "good, clean copy" in no time at all and have it on the editor's desk well before whatever deadline he'd been given. A very light touch of the red pen and the piece would go to press virtually unchanged and everyone would live happily ever after, right? At this point in the story, everyone breathed a sigh and basked in the reflected good feelings of the end of a successful publishing story. And then out of nowhere, the writer thumped the table, shaking everyone out of their reverie. "No!" he shouted. "That's just the beginning."

You see, the writer saw himself as not that far removed from the average local corner-store owner, except for the fact that the corner-store guy had ice cream, canned soup, and toilet paper behind his counter, and the writer had words and ideas, metaphors and imagery, and figures of speech in his storeroom. But they both wanted the same thing—to sell their stock. But once the corner store had sold a container of ice cream, that was it; that ice cream was gone forever. But the writer is not actually selling his words. He retains ownership of his words and licenses the right for someone to use them in a specific geographic territory for a specific period of time. And only that. Nothing more. Which means if his article is sold in one city—let's say Melbourne, to use an Australian example—it can't be sold to papers in Sydney or Brisbane or Canberra, as there are syndication deals in place for those cities, but it doesn't mean it can't be sold in Adelaide or Perth or Darwin. And once the local market is exhausted, then the article can be sold to the UK or the United States or New Zealand. I remember him talking about a weekly column that he wrote for a series of newspapers in New Zealand, the United States, and England—exactly the same column, word for word. As he said, "You could write the column for one client and earn $500 for it, or you could do exactly the same amount of work and earn $1,500. Which would you rather do?" He told us about one article that was proudly celebrating its twenty-first birthday. He'd been publishing it for twenty-one years! Never the same article twice, of course—he'd tweak it, localize it, bring it up-to-date. But essentially the same piece of research and writing being exploited, in a positive sense.

Being a professional in this field isn't going to be easy. It's hard enough coming up with interesting and creative ideas for your content, but then you actually have to find the self-motivation, commitment, and time management skills to write them—and then you have to sell them. But essentially you just have to get on with it. If you need good advice, just google legendary Canadian writer Margaret Atwood. She has been very generous with her words of wisdom and inspiration for writers, but they are always really grounded and down to earth. I especially love the quote that ends with "so don't whine." No sugar-coating there! So like Margaret said: don't whine. Just get on with it!

30

SHOULD I GET AN AGENT?

Whenever I teach, this question is always asked,
so I am going to answer it now instead of waiting
for you to raise your hands at the end.

There are a couple of different sorts of agents you could be thinking about here. Let's start with literary agents. If you have your first book manuscript ready to go, do you really need a literary agent? As rare as publishers are, agents are even rarer. You could invest a lot of time and energy in finding yourself an agent, or, I would suggest, you could use the same time and energy to find yourself a publisher or even just get on with your writing.

Also, as the author of a nonfiction book, possibly in the early stages of your literary career, there's actually not a huge amount a literary agent can negotiate for you. You're a smart person, and it wouldn't take much for you to read and understand a publishing contract and to make suggestions or requests of your publisher to get all the *t*'s crossed and the *i*'s dotted just how you want them. And if you're getting, say, a $6,000 advance on your book—just to use a nice round number divisible by three for purposes of illustration—an agent could negotiate something like $2,000 on contract signing, $2,000 on manuscript delivery, and the last $2,000 on publication of the book. But then so could you. At this stage of your writing career, an agent may be taking 15 percent of your already fairly small earnings to do something that you're capable of doing yourself.

There is one tiny proviso to all this, however; where I am writing this in sunny Australia, this is pretty much how it is. On the other hand, over in the States where you are probably reading this, the publishing industry is a little more reluctant to look at work by unagented writers. And your gene pool of agents is considerably larger than ours. It's just a "size of the country, size of the industry" thing. I still think a smart person can tackle this on their own and get their manuscript, or at least a sample of it, under the eyes of a publisher, but if you do get anywhere near an agent who looks vaguely interested in you, please don't say, "No, thanks; Mr. Clews said I didn't need you."

Once you get onto your second and third books, however, the story changes—especially if the book or books that preceded them were reasonably successful. At this point, an agent can be much more useful to you. Not only would you be more in demand as an author, having proved your worth with solid sales and a bit of visibility, but they'd have more to play with in terms of negotiation—amount of advance, timing of payment, and so on—given that third and fourth books by a successful author tend to attract higher returns. Keep going like that and you might find it'll be the agents who are seeking you out.

What could be quite useful to you to begin with, however, is a speakers' agent who can help find you work as a speaker, presenter, and public figure. If you have already published a book, your book publicist might arrange speaking engagements, but these will be all about marketing your book when it comes out. A speakers' agency is more likely to arrange appearances in schools to talk about your work, maybe even giving demonstrations or practical workshops, where the emphasis is on the performance or experience. A speakers' agent will be looking for gigs that attract a fee, whereas your publicist's eye is on the book sales, in the short and long term. As with all agents, of course, a speakers' agent will be looking for something to work with, so you'll need a successful commercial publication record or a decent profile before one will take you on.

Now, of course, you can arrange author appearances yourself if you want to, but what you'll quickly find out if you decide to have a go at this is that it's all about relationships. Where speakers' agents— and publicists too, for that matter—are brilliant is in their contact lists. Relationships take time—sometimes years, even—to develop, but the payoff once you gain someone's trust is unbeatable. That trust will get you booked into the same venue to present for years and years and years. Conversely, if you decide to try a little cold-calling yourself, expect to have the door slammed shut in your face— metaphorically speaking, of course—on more than a few occasions. If you do decide to seek out an agent, make sure you do your homework and choose wisely. There are industry associations that many of them—certainly the good ones—belong to, and often they have codes of conduct they sign up to. And there is always the ever-reliable internet and good old-fashioned word of mouth. It's not hard to do a basic background check on someone these days.

However, one golden and, to my mind, unbreakable rule is this: if anyone approaches you and asks you for money at any stage of the process—to read your writing, edit your work, or, in this case, represent you in any way—just walk away. That person is closer to being a predator than a business partner. All good agents make their money by sharing in your success and by taking a relatively small percentage of your income for their part in making you successful. If anyone suggests any other financial arrangement to you, you really don't want to have anything to do with them.

31
WHAT NOW?

Where to next? How to put into practice
what we've talked about—maybe even a
little strategic planning, perhaps?

You can (and, I believe, should) have a go at everything you have read about in this book. Nothing is beyond you; nothing requires extra knowledge—certainly nothing that you can't pick up along the way—or special permission. You already have the authority and credibility you need, and I think you owe it to the rest of us to share your amazing discoveries and insight.

So what should you do next? Here's an idea: why not get strategic and set yourself some goals? Sketch out the year ahead, put in any major projects or time commitments you have, then start adding a few engagement or writing activities. Of course, you can't guarantee the outcome of these—you can pitch a story, for example, but only an editor can decide to publish it—but you should at least try. And it goes without saying that the more you try, the greater your chances of succeeding are. But even if you start modestly, you could aim for at least one story on your work or a small profile piece in the local paper, one story by you about your research in a slightly higher-profile publication, a couple of radio appearances—one community and one national—and maybe a gig onstage at a midrange writers' or ideas festival. You could even go crazy and come up with a five- or ten-year plan if you like. That's entirely up to you. But you really should try to do something, and the best way of ensuring that you stick to this goal is to have a plan.

Need a quick recap? OK.

Start by making sure you have a **digital footprint** of some sort. Remember: everything from this moment on hinges on people being able to find you. Make sure you are googleable!

Next, how about you get out there and start **talking to people** about what you do?

Within academia, there are some great **competitions** to get you started—the Three Minute Thesis, Visualise Your Thesis, Falling Walls Venture, and Fresh Science competitions, to name but a few. My personal passion is the Three Minute Thesis competition—if you need motivation and inspiration and good ideas about how to talk about research topics in a very short time, just watch some of the winning entries from around the world.

But try to go beyond your peers, colleagues, and fellow research-ers. I think you should be **talking to strangers outside the academic system** who don't know you or your work. At the time of writing, we are all hiding away from COVID-19, but before you know it, every day in every major town and city on this planet, there will be groups of people listening to after-dinner speakers. There will be community centers and neighborhood houses running forums and discussion groups. There will be issue-based panels and public meetings. There will be TED and TEDx talks. And if things revert to "normal," there will be enough festivals of every genre imaginable out there to sink a battleship. Make contact, put your name forward, tell them who you are and what you know, and offer yourself to them. You probably won't start center stage, but there's nothing wrong with cutting your teeth as a host or facilitator. Do that well, and soon, you'll be an interviewer and ultimately a panelist and presenter.

Then try getting your name into **print**. Pitch a few stories, starting small with a local publication or community forum, and build up from there. And be persistent. Often, it's just persistence that gets you success, rather than luck or even, dare I say it, talent. But before you know it, your local media will be seeking your comments. Which means you are now a go-to person. Congratulations!

And after that, it's up to you. Take a look at what someone like Alain de Botton has achieved by combining intelligence and creativity with a highly strategic approach to life. He is a great writer, a scintillating public speaker, and a sought-after public commentator; he founded his own answer to the traditional university system, called the School of Life; and he is a great onscreen presenter in television shows based on his own books—television shows produced by his own production company! Very cleverly, he has become his own one-stop shop.

So what are you waiting for? Just do it. I wish you well with the exciting journey you are about to embark on, and I look forward to following your blog, reading your articles, buying your books, and standing in line for the keynote presentation that one day you will be invited to give. You'll see me: I'll be there in the front row, dead center, sitting up straight and smiling maniacally like a proud parent.

32

JUST BEFORE YOU GO

A few last thoughts and some resources that might help you on the next stage of your journey (not that I'd ever use a cliché like "journey").

Here, for your information and reading pleasure, are a few books I'd recommend for writing, presenting, and generally engaging more widely and one or two other useful resources. I'm going to keep the list fairly short—it's more of a short, curated learning experience than an exhaustive bibliographic adventure.

Let's start with a few books that started life as academic research, some of them even as parts of a PhD (not that you'd ever know from reading them). This is a bit of a biased list, as I was there at the start of all these books, standing proudly in the wings, but they represent a nice cross section of the different ways that research can be transformed into highly readable books through good writing, a sense of imagination, and some effective storytelling. *Georgette Heyer's Regency World* by Jennifer Kloester, Idan Ben-Barak's *Small Wonders*, Fraser MacDonald's *Escape from Earth*, *The UFO Diaries* by Martin Plowman, *Our Girls* by Madeleine Hamilton, and *Human*

Remains by Helen MacDonald all started their lives in a modest way on a university campus and then went on to achieve great things all around the world. And they are all highly enjoyable reads.

After that, I think no education in communicating research-driven work is complete without a quick look at the world of creative nonfiction. While not grounded in academic research, these books all represent many hours of exhaustive investigation by authors whose talents include the ability to really bring a story to life, but above all, they are all a "good read." So put your feet up, and be inspired by how enthralling nonfiction at its best can be.

One of the first bestsellers in this field was *In Cold Blood* by Truman Capote; often referred to as the first "nonfiction novel," this book has sold millions, was filmed twice, and is still in print well over half a century after its initial publication. Definitely worth a look just to see how a mostly true factual account can be brought to life on the page.

When I was at the helm of the Melbourne Writers Festival, I was lucky enough to experience a golden age in creative nonfiction. So many brilliant books came out within a relatively short period of time, so if you have a moment to yourself and need a spot of inspiration, look out for Simon Winchester's *The Map that Changed the World*, James McBride's *The Color of Water*, *Longitude* by Dava Sobel, anything by David Crystal on language, *Big Chief Elizabeth* by Giles Milton, *E=mc²* by David Bodanis, *Wild Swans* by Jung Chang, *The Code Book* by Simon Singh, *The Dinosaur Hunters* by Deborah Cadbury, and pretty much anything by Erik Larson—a writer who is as close to being an academic researcher as you'll find in the outside world. And my personal favorite, John Berendt's *Midnight in the Garden of Good and Evil*, while not a research-based title, is such an enthralling and imaginatively written memoir that many an interviewer—myself included—accidentally referred to it as a novel.

Creative nonfiction continues to hold its own consistently in the bestseller lists. To pick a few recommendations: *The Information* by James Gleick, *The Sixth Extinction* by Elizabeth Kolbert, *Stuff Matters* by Mark Miodownik, *The Battle for God* by Karen Armstrong, *Rats* by Robert Sullivan, *The Immortal Life of Henrietta Lacks* by Rebecca Skloot, and Bill Bryson's fact-filled *A Short History of Nearly Everything*. John Lewis's *March* trilogy takes this genre into the relatively rare world of graphic memoir, and, of course, any of Toni Morrison's nonfiction writing will take your breath away.

I've already mentioned the work of Professor Inger Mewburn from the Australian National University, probably better known to the world as the Thesis Whisperer. I don't just want to point you towards Inger's books, which are fascinating and eminently readable, but also suggest you take a look at her overall brand. The Thesis Whisperer is as close as you can get to a household name in PhD circles, and the very clever ways in which Inger has interwoven both the personal and the professional into her highly impressive empire are well worth learning from.

In my view, reading good writing and seeking inspiration from it is the best way to improve your writing, but there are a few how-to-write books you might want to glance at. *On Writing Well* by William Zinsser is worth a look, and there is a mighty tome called *The Portable MFA in Creative Writing* put out by the New York Writers Workshop that crams everything you could ever want to know about writing but couldn't afford the tuition fees to learn into one fairly chunky volume. There aren't that many physical copies of it left, but it's definitely out there in the digital domain. I've also mentioned John Birmingham and *How to Be a Writer Who Smashes Deadlines, Crushes Editors, and Lives in a Solid Gold Hovercraft*. Not only is this a hugely practical book—from an author whose feet are firmly on the ground—but it's also a great demonstration of the effectiveness of dictation software, which injury first forced John to use but which he swears by now.

You'll also find the odd event or two on campus or on your local writers' festival program that will help you on this exciting journey. Anything that offers training in communication and engagement is worth a look, as are pitch panels and pitching workshops run by people like the Australian Society of Authors over here, or the American Society of Journalists and Authors where you are. And science communication is all the rage at the moment, so maybe see if you can find something in this field that you can adapt to your own discipline.

The other thing to look out for are writing and publishing conferences and events, particularly what are called pitch conferences. You get to work on your pitch or query letter, often with the help of some highly qualified people, and at the end of the event the lucky ones get to deliver that pitch to real life publishing industry representatives. There are plenty of these around all over the world but my favourite by far is the one produced four times a year (two fiction, two nonfiction) by the New York Writers Workshop. Sure, you need to save up a tiny bit for New York airfare and a few nights' accommodation, but you will learn from the best, see a whole host of other writers in action, and come out with a clear and concise pitch for a book that you will get to pitch to two or three big-name publishers. What's not to love about that?

And remember that YouTube can be your friend. If you want to become a better communicator, there are enough TED Talks and Three Minute Thesis presentations out there to give you a lifetime's worth of inspiration.

And that's it. That's all you need to know to become a "new academic." What you have to do now is put it into practice. Have a good look at your expertise, and work out what you've got to say. Decide who you'd like to talk to, and then get going. It really is as simple as that. Sure you'll make mistakes along the way—we all do—but you'll also learn quickly, and before you know it, you'll be dashing off articles by the dozen and wowing huge audiences with your charismatic presentations. If you choose to become a new academic, the rest of us get to benefit from your research and your ideas, and the world becomes a better place. And that is definitely a story with a happy ending.

REFERENCES
AND RESOURCES

REFERENCES

ABC Radio National. "Can Better Science Communication Help Counter Pseudoscience?" *Big Ideas.* November 18, 2019 https://www.abc.net.au/radionational/programs/bigideas/enhancing-public-awareness-and-knowledge-of-science/11694100.

Atwood, Margaret. "Margaret Atwood's Rules for Writing." *Guardian*, February 22, 2010. https://www.theguardian.com/books/2010/feb/22/margaret-atwood-rules-for-writers.

Banks, Kirsten, (@astrokirsten). TikTok. https://www.tiktok.com/@astrokirsten.

Carter, Howard, and A. C. Mace. *The Tomb of Tut-Ankh-Amen: Discovered by the Late Earl of Carnarvon and Howard Carter.* London: Cassell, 1923.

Crystal, David, interview by Nora Young. "Aphorism and Tweeting, Internet Linguistics, Visual Effects, Tom Green vs. the Web, and

Duque, Lina. "How Academics and Researchers Can Get More out of Social Media." *Harvard Business Review.* June 8, 2016. https://hbr.org/2016/06/how-academics-and-researchers-can-get-more-out-of-social-media.

Fahy, Eamonn. "2015 3MT Grand Final—Eamonn Fahy" University of Melbourne. September 7, 2015 YouTube video, 3:06, https://youtu.be/NexaXEPL3lg.

Grobel, Lawrence. *Conversations with Capote.* New York: New American Library, 1985.

King, Stephen, quoted in Maggie Zhang. "22 Lessons from Stephen King on How to Be a Great Writer" *Business Insider* August 12, 2014. https://www.businessinsider.com.au/stephen-king-on-how-to-write-2014-8.
——— *On Writing: A Memoir of the Craft*. New York: Scribner, 2000.
Mewburn, Inger. "What Not to Wear: The Academic Edition." *The Thesis Whisperer* (blog). April 16, 2012. https://thesiswhisperer.com/2012/04/16/what-not-to-wear-the-academic-edition/.
Pollitt, Rachel. "Mathematics and Assessment in Early Childhood Education." ePoster Competition 2017 Gallery, University of Melbourne https://library.unimelb.edu.au/research/visualise-your-thesis/gallery/eposter-competition-2017-gallery.
Self, Will "Will Self's Rules for Writers." *Guardian*. February 23, 2010 https://www.theguardian.com/books/2010/feb/22/will-self-rules-for-writers.
Smith, Zadie "That Crafty Feeling" *The Believer*. June 1, 2008 https://believermag.com/that-crafty-feeling/.Young, Nora, interviewing David Crystal. "Aphorism and Tweeting, Internet Linguistics, Visual Effects, Tom Green vs. the Web, and Service Design.'''' Spark. June 9, 2013. https://www.cbc.ca/radio/spark/aphorism-and-tweeting-internet-linguistics-visual-effects-tom-green-vs-the-web-and-service-design-1.1527659.

EDITING AND WRITING RESOURCES

McKenzie, Margaret. *Handbook for Writers and Editors: Grammar, Usage and Punctuation*, 3rd ed. Melbourne: Dundas Press, 2004.
(A good, solid textbook for those for whom the English language is a tool of their trade.)
Strunk, William, Jr., and E. B. White. *The Elements of Style*, 4th ed. New York: Pearson, 2019.
(Whether you use this as a reference or just read it out of pure interest, no writer's bookshelf is complete without Strunk and White. Even the evolution of the various editions of the book tells a great story of language development.)
Tredinnick, Mark. *The Little Green Grammar Book*. Sydney: University of New South Wales Press, 2009.
———. *The Little Red Writing Book*. Sydney: University of New South Wales Press, 2006.
(It's been a while since Mark Tredinnick wrote these, but you can still find them on sale, they will teach you lots, and they won't break the bank.)
Truss, Lynne. *Eats, Shoots & Leaves*. New York: HarperCollins, 2009.
(And as a bit of a grammar Nazi myself, I'd say it's still hard to go past this one, both a collection of interesting thoughts on grammar and a good example of someone turning their personal obsession into a nonfiction bestseller.)

OTHER RESOURCES

American Society of Journalists and Authors, asja.org/.

The Literary Marketplace, literarymarketplace.com/.

COMPETITIONS

Falling Walls Venture competition, falling-walls.com/.

Three Minute Thesis competition, threeminutethesis.uq.edu.au/.

Visualise Your Thesis competition, sites.research.unimelb.edu.au/visualise-your -thesis/home.

EVENTS

New York Writers Workshop Pitch Conference, newyorkwritersworkshop.com /non-fiction-pitch-conference

APPENDICES

SAMPLE INVOICE

INVOICE

From: Your name, address, city, zip code

ABN: 1234567890 (or whatever business registration details you use in your home territory)

To: The client organization, their address, city, and zip code

Attention: Your contact there, with their department and job title if they have one

Invoice No: I use the year, the month, the day, and then a number to distinguish individual invoices if I issue more than one a day, so the first invoice I send on May 24, 2022 becomes 20220524-01

Date: The date you issue the invoice

For: What you've done for the money they are paying you—be as specific as you can with descriptions, dates, etc.

Amount:

Item one	$500
Item two	$500
Item three	$2,000

TOTAL DUE	**$3,000**

Signed:

**Checks should be made payable to
"YOUR ACCOUNT NAME"**

**Direct credit should go to
YOUR BANK NAME account as follows:**

B.S.B. 000 000

ACC. NO. 000 000

ACC. NAME Your account name

SAMPLE PITCH

This is the pitch for the story I mentioned at the end of "Newspapers and Magazines." To give a little background: I quite liked to travel to Singapore (it was a sentimental favorite, as it was the first place I ever got to teach internationally, and, of course, there's always all that shopping and dining just begging to be done), and I knew that the fiftieth anniversary of the founding of the city-state was coming up. Sounded like a good idea for a story to me! So I put together the pitch below and sent it in. Interestingly, while I didn't send it to the opinion pages but saw it as more of a feature or background briefing to a news item, it ended up being published on the opinion pages.

Dear...,

I'd like to run an idea for a piece I'd like to write past you. If you could have a look and let me know if you'd be interested in taking it, I'd be grateful.

I'm an academic specialist at Melbourne University teaching engagement and written and oral communication to researchers there. I often jump on a plane and teach overseas, and Singapore is one of my favorite places to visit—I'll be there later this month on what I think is my twenty-sixth visit (although I must admit I have lost count). [Here I mentioned the writing I'd done before for similar publications, in a sentence, and ended it with this:] You can read more about me at www.simonclews.com.

August 9 will see the city-state of Singapore celebrate fifty years since its founding. Each year, National Day, as it is known, is a huge celebration—it's something like

Australia Day meets the Edinburgh military tattoo with a dose of Mardi Gras thrown in for good measure. The National Day Parade is a nation-stopping event that will be significant this year not only because of the country's half century but also because this will be the first such event since the death of the country's founding father, Lee Kuan Yew.

I'd like to write a piece that takes the parade as its starting point (I have a media pass that allows me in to observe the dress rehearsal) and then explores how far the country has come in fifty years. I'll talk to a few of the locals and ask them about the day, its significance, and where they think the country is headed.

I anticipate writing around eight hundred words and would finish the piece over there the day after the parade and have it to you probably the day after that. Given that the dress rehearsal is the weekend before, you'd then be able to publish the piece on August 9—National Day.

I'd be keen to hear what you think.
With best wishes,
Simon Clews

And that was it—short, sharp, and to the point. I tell them who I am, I throw in a bit of background so they know I can write and have a good chance of delivering on time and word count, and then I give them the flavor of the story. That's all you need. They must have liked it, as you can see from the result: "Singapore at 50: Doing Whatever It Takes to Succeed," *Sydney Morning Herald*, August 6, 2015,

smh.com.au/opinion/singapore-at-50-doing-whatever-it-takes-to
-succeed-20150803-giq47h.html.

SAMPLE MEDIA RELEASE

Remember the smart people I mentioned at the start of the book? This is them in action. In January 2020, the Doherty Institute were the first people outside China to grow and share the COVID-19 virus. When they told the world about what they had done, this is what they sent to the media:

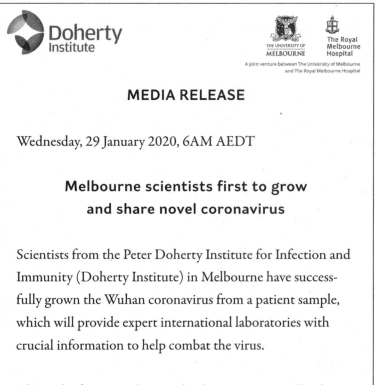

MEDIA RELEASE

Wednesday, 29 January 2020, 6AM AEDT

Melbourne scientists first to grow and share novel coronavirus

Scientists from the Peter Doherty Institute for Infection and Immunity (Doherty Institute) in Melbourne have success-fully grown the Wuhan coronavirus from a patient sample, which will provide expert international laboratories with crucial information to help combat the virus.

This is the first time the virus has been grown in cell culture outside of China.

The Royal Melbourne Hospital's Dr Julian Druce, Virus Identification Laboratory Head at the Doherty Institute, said this was a significant breakthrough as it will allow accurate investigation and diagnosis of the virus globally.

"Chinese officials released the genome sequence of this novel coronavirus, which is helpful for diagnosis, however, having the real virus means we now have the ability to actually validate and verify all test methods, and compare their sensitivities and specificities—it will be a game changer for diagnosis," Dr Druce said.

"The virus will be used as positive control material for the Australian network of public health laboratories, and also shipped to expert laboratories working closely with the World Health Organization (WHO) in Europe."

Dr Mike Catton, Deputy Director of the Doherty Institute, said that possession of a virus isolate extended what could be achieved with molecular technology in the fight against this virus.

The Doherty Institute–grown virus is expected to be used to generate an antibody test, which allows detection of the virus in patients who haven't displayed symptoms and were therefore unaware they had the virus.

"An antibody test will enable us to retrospectively test

suspected patients so we can gather a more accurate picture of how widespread the virus is, and consequently, among other things, the true mortality rate," said Dr Catton.

"It will also assist in the assessment of effectiveness of trial vaccines."

The virus was grown from a patient sample that arrived at the Royal Melbourne Hospital's Victorian Infectious Diseases Reference Laboratory (VIDRL) at the Doherty Institute on Friday, 24 January.

ACKNOWLEDGMENTS

There are so many people I should thank for inspiring me to write this book, but the sad fact is that I've forgotten most of their names. I have, however, remembered their research topics, their expert knowledge and specializations, and all the amazing anecdotes that brought their work to life over the last decade and a half of teaching in universities around the world. So thanks to them, I can warn you about the dangers of the Hendra virus (watch out for those bats!), I can tell you why airplanes make the noise they do as they traverse the skies (it's the flame you can hear), and I can regale people at dinner parties with the astonishing capacity of some people to actually hear colors (although saying "synesthesia" toward the end of a dinner party can sometimes be a bit of a challenge).

The good people at NewSouth in Australia should be thanked for taking the brave, some would say crazy decision to originally publish this book, as should everyone at Sourcebooks for continuing the insanity and indulging me even more with this exciting U.S. edition.

In "Should I Get an Agent?", the one answer I didn't give there is "No—not if you've got a very good friend who is one." Clare Forster is one of the best literary agents in Australia and—for me at least—the font of all knowledge as far as the publishing process is concerned.

And if ever I want to know how books are sold, I always turn to Mary Dalmau, now busy making sure the legal profession all sit up and pay attention, but prior to that for more years than she probably cares to count, Australia's most experienced and successful bookseller.

"Less Is More" explains how writing is at the very most 49 percent of the process to editing's 51 percent; well, my 51 percent (and probably a great deal more) was Emma Driver for the first Australian edition, without whom this book might well have been a series of incoherent ramblings, and now Kate Roddy and Emily Proano at Sourcebooks, who have continued the eagle-eyed oversight. Here's a little inside writing tip—get yourself some of these editors with their big red pens, and their fancy gerunds and Chicago referencing systems, and people will think you really know how to write. It worked for me!

Lastly, but definitely not least, a special thank-you to all the people at home and abroad, in classrooms, hotels, and Qantas lounges, who have been ignored or who have had to wait "just one more minute" while I finished a sentence, a paragraph, or a chapter. For meetings that have been postponed, dinners that have been served late, and dogs that someone else has had to walk, apologies. It won't happen again. Until the next book, of course.

INDEX

ABOUT THE AUTHOR

© *Kai Clews*

Simon Clews was the inaugural Director of the Melbourne Engagement Lab at Australia's Melbourne University, where for fifteen years he enhanced the reputation of a world-leading and innovative university through training, encouraging, and facilitating some of Australia's brightest minds to make their work accessible to non-academic audiences. He then took the show on the road and these days— pandemics permitting—can usually be found wandering the world turning researchers and academics into inspiring communicators. He also works with professional writers helping them hone their craft and is one of the world's most experienced literary and ideas-based event organizers. He is the author of the Australian edition of *The New Academic* (NewSouth Books) and *Your Time Starts Now!* (Thesis Whisperer Books), as well as a long lost and mercifully forgotten book on mail order shopping, *Let's Go Shopping* (Mandarin).

For more information visit simonclews.com.